BLIND DEMOCRACY
The Shame of Hypocrisy

Copyright ©2023 by Captain D. Terry Yarbrough (RET.)
All rights reserved.

No part of this book may be used or reproduced, stored, or transmitted in any form or by any means, electronic, mechanical, photocopying, recording, scanning, or otherwise without written permission. It is illegal to copy this book, post it to a website, or distribute it by any other means without permission. The stories in this book reflect the author's recollection of events. Many names, locations, and identifying characteristics have been changed to protect the privacy of those depicted. Dialogue has been recreated from memory.

Book and Cover design by Pamela D. Cox
ISBN: 978-1-7377017-2-9 Print
ISBN: 978-1-7377017-3-6 Ebook
First Edition
Printed in the United States of America.

Scriptures are taken from the KING JAMES VERSION (KJV):
KING JAMES VERSION, public domain.

Note: *The author recommends that readers read the original news articles represented by italicized excerpts throughout the book.*

BLIND DEMOCRACY
The Shame of Hypocrisy

"Hating people because of their color is wrong. And it doesn't matter which color does the hating. It's just plain wrong."
— Muhammad Ali

"History is not the past. It is the present. We carry our history with us. We are our history."
— James Baldwin

"Pit race against race, religion against religion, prejudice against prejudice. Divide and conquer! We must not let that happen here."
— Eleanor Roosevelt

BLIND DEMOCRACY
The Shame of Hypocrisy

"The Struggle Continues for Civil Rights in AMERICAN DEMOCRACY"

July 2, 1964 -- President Lyndon Johnson signs the Civil Rights Act of 1964. You may recognize the civil rights leader directly behind Johnson—it's Martin Luther King, Jr. The other African Americans in the photo are Ralph Abernathy (covered directly behind King) and John Lewis (to the left of Abernathy). PHOTOGRAPH BY CECIL STOUGHTON, WHITE HOUSE PRESS OFFICE

BLIND DEMOCRACY
The Shame of Hypocrisy

Captain D. Terry Yarbrough, (Retired)
Shelby County Sheriff's Office
Memphis, Tennessee
FBINA 187

In America, law enforcement officers swear by oath to uphold the United States Constitution and Rule of Law, regardless of race, ethnicity, or skin color. The Constitution represents the supreme law of the land. *Trust, integrity,* and *respect* are fundamental values required to ensure *accountability, transparency,* and *fairness* in performing duties and enforcing applicable laws and policies.

As a Black American, my law enforcement career resulted in challenging lessons learned: *What to do, How to do,* and *What not to do.* Perhaps, many of my peers, locally and abroad, experienced similar lessons. I served 16 years as a Memphis police officer and 28 years as a deputy sheriff in Shelby County, Tennessee, earning the rank of Captain. I learned that *character, integrity,* and *intellect* are winning attributes for success in professional law enforcement. The same holds true for success in any lawful profession.

John Q. Public often misunderstands the complex realities of professional policing, notably misguided citizens who rush to judgment with misplaced emotions or false assumptions. Many law enforcement officers are misguided, too. I speak with the weapon of truth, unabashed by what others think, even though it might sound like hogwash to those comfortable denying or misrepresenting the truth.

-- *DTY*

GOD is my strength and power:
And HE maketh my way perfect.
2 Samuel 22:33 KJV

Table of Contents

ACKNOWLEDGEMENT 9

PROLOGUE 11

PREFACE 13

INTRODUCTION 19

    1 The Sad Truth 35

    2 Audacity of Hypocrisy 47

    3 Believe It, or Not 63

    4 Policing Culture 73

    5 Training Culture 83

    6 Hearts & Minds 99

    7 Now Is the Time 107

    8 Implicit Bias 117

    9 "Wake Up, America" 135

REFERENCES 157

ABOUT THE AUTHOR 163

ACKNOWLEDGEMENT

"Service to Mankind is the Rent We Pay for Our Room Here on Earth." -- Anonymous

I proudly honor good Police Officers or "Good Apples" in America for meritorious service to humanity. "We, the People," must support the good police officers who command authority with *courage, respect,* and *integrity.* Honorable men and women risk their lives to serve and protect with the highest standards of ethical conduct. I am eternally grateful.

In denouncing "Bad Apples," I introduced news perspectives and job experiences exposing *racial hypocrisy, political extremism,* and *implicit bias* that undermine American Democracy and Law Enforcement.

GOOD APPLES:
Sworn to uphold Democracy,
Disavowing Hypocrisy.
Willing to serve and protect,
Always without neglect.

No doubt,
Moving out and about.
Right on time,
Rain or shine.
With much blame,
Staying in the game.
Never serving for fame,
Protecting just the same.

Serving modestly,
Obeying the law and policy.
Eager to learn and train,
Choosing not to complain.

BAD APPLES:
No mistrust or fuss,
Moral integrity is a must.
Face the change.
Erase your bad name.
-- DTY

"So, I have tried to make it clear that it is wrong to use immoral means to attain moral ends. But now I must affirm that it is just as wrong, or even more so, to use moral means to preserve immoral ends." -- Dr. Martin Luther King, Jr.

PROLOGUE

We, the People, must embrace AMERICAN DEMOCRACY and the Rule of Law for the prosperity of all citizens, regardless of race, ethnicity, gender, skin color, or political affiliation.

In 1863, the 16th president of the United States of America, Abraham Lincoln, defined Democracy as the *"Government of the people for the people and by the people."* Unity of democracy is a shared commitment to guarantee freedom, liberty, and justice. According to an Old English Proverb, *"What is good for the goose is good for the gander."*

The United States of America comprises a multiracial, multicultural blend of free-thinking people ruled by Representative Democracy and the Rule of Law, not *hypocrisy, extremism,* and *hatred.* Subsequently, the institution of Law Enforcement should govern accordingly with best practices.

Law enforcement officers should uphold Democracy. They are not above the Rule of Law, nor are they the lawmakers; they enforce the law with the highest standards of professional and ethical conduct.

Misguided police officers, politicians, criminal justice professionals, clergy members, educators, and citizens radicalized by extremist ideology will self-destruct. Many find it challenging to embrace human rights and equal justice for people of color, notably Black people.

As stewards of American Democracy, public servants and religious leaders must model and practice what they preach. Truth, trust, and integrity are paramount. Dr. Martin Luther King, Jr. reminded us, *"Nothing in the World Is More Dangerous Than Sincere Ignorance and Conscientious Stupidity."*

PREFACE

*T*he following excerpt distinguishes a speech delivered by FREDERICK DOUGLASS on July 5, 1852, at Corinthian Hall in Rochester, New York, during a meeting organized by the Rochester Ladies' Anti-Slavery Society. Douglass rebuked the "Fourth of July" holiday and the racial hypocrisy manifested in American Democracy.

Source:
TIME MAGAZINE / July 03, 2019 / Updated June 26, 2020
'What to the Slave Is the Fourth of July?': The History of Frederick Douglass' Searing Independence Day Oration
By Olivia B. Waxman

> *"What, to the American slave, is your Fourth of July? I answer: a day that reveals to him, more than all other days in the year, the*

gross injustice and cruelty to which he is the constant victim. To him, your celebration is a sham; your boasted liberty, an unholy license; your national greatness, swelling vanity; your sounds of rejoicing are empty and heartless; your denunciations of tyrants, brass-fronted impudence; your shouts of liberty and equality, hollow mockery; your prayers and hymns, your sermons and thanksgivings, with all your religious parade, and solemnity, are, to him, mere bombast, fraud, deception, impiety, and hypocrisy— a thin veil to cover up crimes which would disgrace a nation of savages. There is not a nation on the earth guilty of practices more shocking and bloodier than are the people of these United States at this very hour." -- Frederick Douglass

As the author of "BLIND DEMOCRACY: *The Shame of Hypocrisy,*" a sequel to "MISGUIDED BADGES: *A Personal Memoir,*" like Frederick Douglass, I aim to unmask the assumed *patriotism* and *exceptionalism* boasted in American Democracy. I proclaim no ulterior motive, only to speak the truth. My loyalty to America's constitutional beliefs, principles, and values is unwavering.

The book exposes the influence of *racial hypocrisy, political extremism,* and *implicit bias* in Democracy and Law Enforcement. News excerpts, facts, and opinions are asserted to raise awareness, reconcile differences, and encourage racial healing. For years, misguided police officers and unethical politicians blindfolded Democracy with *mistrust, misuse of authority,* and *abusive practices.*

"Blind Democracy" portrays *White Supremacy* and *White Privilege* as defiant of human rights and equal justice for all in America, the sweet land of liberty. "Hypocrisy" characterizes the moral compass of public servants, e.g., police officers, politicians, government bureaucrats, criminal justice professionals, educators, and clergy members who say one thing but do another. In addition, hope remains alive for effective change in America's broken policing culture.

OATH of OFFICE
(Sample)

Police Officer

I do solemnly swear that I will support the Constitutions of the United States and of the State of Tennessee, and the ordinances of the City of _____, and will well and faithfully perform the duties imposed upon me as a police officer of the City of _____, to the best of my ability; and that I will serve the United States, the State of Tennessee, and the City of _____ honestly and faithfully, and will obey the orders of the officers and officials placed over me according to law.

Name: _____   Date: _____

Signature: _____

Mayor: _____

Municipal Technical Advisory Services (MTAS)
Reviewed Date: 04/19/2021.
www.mtas.tennessee.edu

IACP LAW ENFORCEMENT CODE OF ETHICS

The IACP adopted the Law Enforcement Code of Ethics at the 64th Annual IACP Conference and Exposition in October 1957. The Code of Ethics stands as a preface to the mission and commitment law enforcement agencies make to the public they serve.

As a law enforcement officer, my fundamental duty is to serve the community; to safeguard lives and property; to protect the innocent against deception, the weak against oppression or intimidation, the peaceful against violence or disorder; and to respect the constitutional rights of all to liberty, equality, and justice.

I will keep my private life unsullied as an example to all and behave in a manner that does not bring discredit to me or my agency. I will maintain courageous calm in the face of danger, scorn, or ridicule; develop self-restraint, and be constantly mindful of the welfare of others. Honest in thought and deed, both in my personal and official life, I will be exemplary in obeying the law and the regulations of my department. Whatever I see or hear of a confidential nature or that is confided to me in my official capacity will be kept secret unless revelation is necessary for the performance of my duty.

I will never act officiously or permit personal feelings, prejudices, political beliefs, aspirations, animosities, or friendships to influence my decisions. With no compromise for crime and with relentless prosecution of criminals, I will enforce the law courteously and appropriately without fear or favor, malice, or ill will, never employing unnecessary force or violence, and never accepting gratuities.

I recognize the badge of my office as a symbol of public faith, and I accept it as a public trust to hold so long as I am true to the ethics of police service. I will never engage in acts of corruption or bribery, nor will I condone such actions by other police officers. I will cooperate with all legally authorized agencies and their representatives in the pursuit of justice.

I know that I alone am responsible for my standard of professional performance and will take every reasonable opportunity to enhance and improve my level of knowledge and competence. I will constantly strive to achieve these objectives and ideals, dedicating myself before God to my chosen profession, law enforcement.

– International Association of Chiefs of Police (IACP)

INTRODUCTION

"**B**LIND DEMOCRACY: *The Shame of Hypocrisy*" is a sequel to "MISGUIDED BADGES: *A Personal Memoir.*" The reader-friendly Memoir features italicized excerpts from news pieces, exposing *Racial Hypocrisy, Political Extremism,* and *Implicit Bias* undermining American Democracy and Law Enforcement. The news perspectives reveal facts and opinions from public sources throughout the book. The eye-opening views and experiences are significant in raising awareness, reconciling differences, and encouraging racial healing.

"Blind Democracy," a cultural shame, is a perpetual enabler of systemic racism coveted by implicit biases of misguided police officers, political extremists, and radicalized citizens. As a result, *Moral Decay,* a national affliction, trends throughout our polarized country, blinding

Democracy with racial hypocrisy, extremism, and hatred.

American Democracy, under the patriotic pretense of *Exceptionalism,* maintains sightless eyes to equal justice for Black citizens. White supremacists strive to advance conspiracy theories and false assumptions with radical agendas. Misguided police officers continue misusing authority and violating the civil rights of citizens who do not look like them. "We, the People," cannot eradicate the racism and extremism that haunt Democracy with deliberate "SILENCE" or "INDIFFERENCE." We must work together and engage seriously in respectful dialogue with common sense for winning outcomes.

White supremacy ideology has grown to sabotage Democracy with violent, treasonous acts of extremism. This egregious behavior includes police misconduct, fatal shootings of innocent school children, hate crimes targeting Black people, Jews, and Asians, and massively assaulting the U.S. Capitol in Washington, DC. The U.S. Department of Justice (DOJ) strives judiciously to prosecute violent extremists with certainty.

America must not look the other way or take for granted the threats of *White Supremacy, White Nationalism,* and *White Christian Nationalism.* The ideal solutions to changing racial extremists' "Hearts & Minds" are fervent prayer, the certainty of prosecution, and unified voting. VOTING is power, period.

Black and brown citizens continually endure racial injustices perpetrated by white supremacists and white nationalists. Misguided law enforcement officers remain center front with this pervasive, radical nonsense. I speak not from hearsay but from what *I read, saw,* and *experienced,* revealing disturbing outcomes. The white supremacy and white nationalism ideology undermining our fragile Democracy constitute a moral reckoning of trust and integrity challenging sheriffs, police chiefs, and politicians nationwide.

Forty-four years of career challenges motivated me to raise awareness of widespread racism and extremism driven by toxic political discourse. I experienced it firsthand as a Black police officer and deputy sheriff in Memphis and Shelby County, Tennessee. I aim to attract attention with the *truth, valid opinions,* and *open communication.*

Let me be clear: *"A new day is upon us in American law enforcement."* Public outcry has increased the call for meaningful changes and reforms. How do *"We, the People,"* navigate them? *Racial Hate* and *Ignorance,* too, have blindfolded misguided law enforcement professionals, elected officials, and radicalized citizens. They fail to see the forest for the trees. We should be outraged by this perverted nonsense propagated to undermine Democracy.

Should we succumb to phony patriotism and political principles, defying common sense, inciting treasonous protest and violence, and destroying the moral consciousness of our democratic nation? Should we spread conspiracy theories, baseless lies, and false assumptions; whitewash Black History with conscientious stupidity; and ban books revealing the truth about American History? Is that the American exceptionalism that symbolizes justice and equality for all citizens under the color of law? I do not think so. Proudly, I chose to share career experiences, facts, opinions, and news perspectives exposing the *"Sad Truth."*

Black History matters. Whitewashing Black History and banning educational books and projects viewed as offensive or uncomfortable to White people is nonsense. Moreover, it is morally repulsive in a multiracial Democracy ruled by a majority vote of *"We, the People."* For this reason, *"We"* cannot discern any COMMON SENSE from this NONSENSE.

Therefore, let us keep Black History alive. It is America's history drenched in blood, sweat, and tears, smeared by human bondage, torment, and death. Enslaved Black people contributed the lion's share of *sweat equity* (physical labor) in building the United States of America into a capitalistic society. The *free labor* of Black people accounted immeasurably for the economic prosperity of White enslavers and landowners throughout the southern states.

Today, we commemorate the human sacrifice and incredible contributions made by Black people with *"the painful truth"* preserving Black History in America. Over the years, stereotypes, tribulations, and injustices Black Americans face speak truth to power, revealing the racial hypocrisy and hatred embedded in Democracy.

The recognition, understanding, and acceptance of Black History is monumental for healing, educating, and unifying future generations. Undoubtedly, there has been significant improvement in race relations in our multiracial, multicultural nation. However, we look forward to more social and political changes with a spirited determination to bridge the racial divide plaguing America. Much work remains.

Sadly, the propensity for power and the defiance of truth have become proverbial trademarks of racial hypocrisy and hatred by misguided state and congressional legislators. Right-wing lawmakers are currently the voting majority or supermajority in most state legislative assemblies across the country. Nevertheless, they continue to support unreasonable laws, undermining common sense gun safety recommendations, and negating the will of *"the People"* to regulate gun access.

The random escalation of violent crime and shooting deaths indicates that gun violence is out of control locally and nationally. Lawmakers must focus on championing the interests, safety, and welfare of *"We, the People"* over partisan political objectives and racial extremism.

COLIN POWELL, a Black man, was an exemplary U.S. Army (4-Star) General-Chief of Staff and U.S. Secretary of State. This honorable military leader and role model exemplified authentic leadership and courage, embodying the highest standards of moral integrity. I applaud General Powell's pointed suggestion of *"sad truth."*

> *"We have come to live in a society based on insults, on lies and on things that just aren't true. It creates an environment where deranged people feel empowered."*
> -- General Colin Powell, U.S. Army (Ret.)

White supremacy ideology runs rampant, assaulting the hallowed principles and values of Democracy declared in the U.S. Constitution and Declaration of Independence. Hate-spewing political rhetoric and egregious police misconduct confirm the rising extremism infiltrating law enforcement agencies and branches of government.

Police officers who violate laws and policies and post racist comments on social media platforms pose a significant risk of undermining public trust. They run the risk of having comments misperceived or taken out of context. Many lose their jobs or suffer stern disciplinary consequences over offensive postings of racial abuse.

According to national news reports, the increase in the excessive force and deadly shootings of unarmed Black victims raises a legitimate question: "*How can police officers build public trust and establish relationships if they cannot be trusted?*"

Source:
THE NATION / November 15, 2022
"White Nationalist Hate Is Infiltrating Our Police"
By Kali Holloway

> *Just as the "bad apples" analogy downplays the systemic rot of racist policing, the "lone wolf" theory of white supremacists in law enforcement belies the institutional reality. Departments with officers bearing "sympathy towards the ideologies of extremism leave us all compromised,"* writes *Georgetown University law professor Vida B. Johnson. "If police departments are complicit in the attack on truth and Democracy, they cannot be trusted to protect the general public"* (Holloway, 2022).

Misguided police officers increasingly post racist and extremist views ignored by sympathetic sheriffs, police chiefs, and union officials. It is alarming.

Something to consider: *"Whatever happened to the moral trust and integrity that embody a police officer's Oath of Office, Code of Ethics, or Code of Honor?"* As public trust and integrity erode in Law Enforcement, so goes our fragile Democracy.

On May 3, 2022, according to the Anti-Defamation League (ADL):

> *Extremists within the ranks can have a dangerous and outsized impact on policing in our communities. By associating with extremist movements or publicly expressing support for these ideologies, members of law enforcement are behaving in a way that directly contradicts their oaths to serve and protect our communities and undermines community safety. Some of these extremist beliefs, notably white supremacist ideologies, place vulnerable populations, including Black people and other people of color, as well as immigrant populations, at greater risk of harm (ADL, 2022).*

On January 6, 2021, insurrectionist groups massively assaulted the U.S. Capitol in Washington, DC. The politically calculated, riotous assault was a real-time revelation for all American citizens. The widespread publicity diminished many citizens' respect and confidence in Law Enforcement.

News sources reported that off-duty police officers or *"Bad Apples"* stormed and vandalized the U.S. Capitol videotaped as members of white supremacy and militia groups. Law enforcement officers who aided and abetted this insurrection violated federal law and their oaths of office. They delivered a treasonous blow to Democracy and public trust, sending shock waves worldwide.

FBI agents searched abroad, identified, and arrested hundreds of responsible insurrectionists, returning them to Washington, DC, to face justice.

The massive assault proved an act of political defiance allegedly orchestrated by radicalized militia groups, politicians, and citizens. As reported, they had no regard for redress or consequence while attempting to overturn the certified results of a presidential election.

This horrendous assault was un-American, condemned by most sheriffs, police chiefs, political officials, and law-abiding citizens. It was bizarre that the 45th President of the United States of America failed to timely speak out to deter the insurrectionists who stormed the U.S. Capitol building to overthrow Democracy.

Source:
THE ELM – VOICES & OPINIONS / July 06, 2021
University of Maryland, Baltimore
"The Hypocrisy of White Supremist and Far-Right Groups"
By Valerie Hughes

> *"These groups call themselves "patriots," and they proclaim to love this country, the American flag, the military, and police. However, the white supremacists who attacked the Capitol building, waving Confederate flags, and flags with Nazi and white supremacy insignia, were the same people making vile threats and statements regarding Colin Kaepernick's decision to kneel during the national anthem in protest of racial injustice and police brutality"* (Hughes, 2021).

> *"They brutally beat the Capitol police, they spat on them, bludgeoned them, sprayed them with toxic bear repellent, and even gouged the eyes of the fallen officers. The worst offense was using the American flag as a weapon; the same flag they claimed to love and worship. The American flag that they said Kaepernick disrespected by kneeling was used as a weapon to brutally attack the police they claimed to support"* (rev. 1992) (Hughes, 2021).

Meanwhile, as a Black police officer and deputy sheriff, I survived a career dominated by white supremacy views, perceiving Black folk as inferior. Public confidence and race perceptions remain hot topics as unarmed Black victims disproportionately pay a deadly price for the *"Miscarriage of Justice"* by misguided police officers.

My opinions and views relate to the title and context of this book. I am not a *racist* or an *extremist* by any imagination.

Nonetheless, I make no excuses for ANY lawbreakers whatsoever.

Law and order, equal justice, and racial decency must prevail in American Democracy. I refuse to *"tap dance"* around critical issues and deny the truth. Nothing is nobler than standing firmly on Godly faith and moral integrity, doing the right thing for the right reasons.

Today, rebellious law enforcement officers and elected officials deliberately ignore the core principles and values enshrined in the United States Constitution, the supreme law of the land. Why?

One of the ideal values of the Declaration of Independence, *"All Men Are Created Equal,"* has been long renounced by right-wing politics. White supremacists continue championing themselves as American patriots due to white privilege and skin color. Question: *"How can white supremacists claim American patriotism, undermine Democracy, and defy Constitutional values -- at the same time?"* *Hypocrisy* and *Ignorance* drive their fanaticism to despicable shame.

The audacity of misguided police officers and elected officials to conspire against Democracy is grossly offensive. My advice: *"They should save themselves from themselves."* I characterize law officers and politicians pretending to uphold the Rule of Law while conspiring against Democracy as treasonous hypocrites.

Too many unethical police commanders and subordinates go unchecked, disregarding laws, policies, and best practices without consequence. They know what is right but are too insistent on maintaining inherent biases and old ways. I view them as unworthy of *"Carrying a Badge,"* flaunting self-righteous morals -- at any cost. Americans must find a rational way to *"agree to disagree"* and vent frustrations civilly and nonviolently.

I contend that America has been the gatekeeper of racial hypocrisy and implicit bias since the Founding Fathers wrote the original Declaration of Independence and the U.S. Constitution. American History sources report that the Founding Fathers were white slaveholders and wealthy landowners.

I suggest, too, that American History will confirm that the Founding Fathers were cruel enslavers beholden to white privilege and self-enrichment. They were never true to human rights and equal justice for Black people as promised – *"for all"* -- by the Declaration of Independence and the U.S. Constitution.

Slavery amounted to materially more than man's cruelty against man. Notably, it sustained the American economy and slaveholders' wealth by exploiting Black people's *physical labor.* As enslavers, the Founding Fathers *lynched, tortured, raped,* and *bred* Black people, robbing them of human rights and dignity. The shameless founders pretended and wrote one thing but conveniently held on to doing another. Today, the exact racial hypocrisy and hatred remain deeply rooted in the psyche of white supremacists throughout our fragile system of Democracy.

Source:
SMITHSONIAN MAGAZINE / November 2002
"Founding Fathers and Slaveholders"
By Stephen E. Ambrose

> *"Let's begin with Thomas Jefferson, because it is he who wrote the words that inspired subsequent generations to make the heroic sacrifices that transformed the words 'All men are created equal' into reality" (Ambrose, 2002).*

> *"Jefferson, like all slaveholders and many other white members of American society, regarded Negroes as inferior, childlike, untrustworthy and, of course, as property. Jefferson, the genius of politics, could see no way for African Americans to live in society as free people. He embraced the worst forms of racism to justify slavery" (Ambrose, 2002).*

On March 20, 2019, William F. Spivey, MEDIUM.com, in his news piece, *"America's Breeding Farms: What History Books Never Told You,"* reminded us about the forced breeding of slaves.

> *"We are taught almost nothing about the breeding farms whose function was to produce as many slaves as possible for the sale and distribution throughout the South to meet their needs. Two of the largest breeding farms were located in Richmond, VA, and the Maryland Eastern-Shore" (Spivey, 2019).*

> *"The slave population of the breeding farm was mostly women and children not old enough to be sold, and a limited number of men whose job was to impregnate as many slave women as possible. The slaves were often given hoods or bags over their heads to keep them from knowing who they were having forced sex with. It could be someone they know, perhaps a niece, aunt, sister, or their own mother" (Spivey, 2019).*

Despite the atrocities of slavery, Jim Crow, and modern-day racism, American citizens – Black, Brown, and White -- must understand that the *Rule of Law is* the bedrock of Democracy and Law Enforcement. It keeps the peace, maintains law and order, and ensures public safety.

Americans must realize, too, that *"Respect for Law & Order"* is incumbent on all citizens.

Sheriffs, police chiefs, supervisors, and subordinates should always follow laws, policies, and best practices as expected. They must be accountable for the *accuracy, transparency,* and *disposition* of calls for service, self-initiated enforcement, preliminary and follow-up investigations, and citizen complaints.

Police misconduct and abusive behavior are unacceptable, period. Consequently, any person found guilty -- in a court of law – of a crime or act of lawlessness should be held accountable and prosecuted as mandated by the applicable law.

IDA B. WELLS once said, *"The way to right wrongs is to turn the light of truth upon them."*

I believe Black police officers and deputy sheriffs, active and retired, locally and abroad, would likely share agreeable opinions if willing to speak out. Nevertheless, many are reluctant to speak out because of apparent backlash or subservient mentalities, e.g., *"Go Along to Get Along."*

Law enforcement officers, politicians, and law-abiding citizens must stay laser-focused on embracing Democracy and enforcing the rule of law. Conspiracy theories should never transcend Democracy. We must confront racial, social, and political differences with common sense instead of incendiary rhetoric and violence.

In the final analysis, I predict misguided law enforcement professionals, unethical politicians, and radicalized citizens who champion white supremacy ideology will self-destruct.

Wake up, Americans, and rise above racial ignorance and political stupidity. Let us stand in unity and decency for human rights and equal justice. Changes in *hearts, minds, attitudes,* and *behaviors* are crucial to building mutual trust and establishing relationships to improve race relations. Genuine political advocates and meaningful social reforms are inevitable in sustaining a brighter future in a growing multiracial, multicultural American Democracy.

My prediction constitutes a reassuring outlook for restoring public trust in American Democracy and Law Enforcement. Moreover, it affirms how *"We, the People,"* must overcome *racial hypocrisy, ignorance,* and *hatred* and do better.

1 The Sad Truth

During a 46-year Law Enforcement career, I survived the *"Sad Truth"* that misguided police officers and unethical politicians undermined American Democracy. I witnessed their unreasonable public interactions with marginalized citizens defy the moral intent and mere essence of Democracy without guilt or shame. I reluctantly tolerated hypocritical die-hards who resisted *equality* and *justice* for persons of color, notably Black people.

Political extremism increasingly infiltrated Law Enforcement and contaminated the *Hearts & Minds* of misguided officers rationalizing white supremacy. Their misguided racial beliefs and views assailed constitutional mandates, civil liberties, and the civil rights of others without consequence.

Source:
MASSACHUSETTS INSTITUTE of TECHNOLOGY / 1995
"Police and Democracy"
By Gary T. Marx

> *"In a democratic society, police must not be a law unto themselves. Despite strong pressures and temptations to the contrary, they are not to act in an explicitly political fashion, nor to serve the partisan interests of the party in power, or the party they would like to see in power. Their purpose must not be to enforce political conformity. Holding unpopular beliefs or behaving in unconventional, yet legal, ways are not adequate grounds for interfering with citizen's liberty. When opponents of Democracy operate within the law police have an obligation to protect their rights, as well as the rights of others (Marx, 1995)."*

The term *"Bad Apples,"* describes police officers who willfully disregard laws, policies, and best practices, violating the Rights of others. They abuse authority with *moral decay* to the detriment of public trust and integrity. Moral decay symbolizes the deterioration of morals, principles, and values in a civil society of free-thinking people.

Morals are core precepts determining choices or preferences of what to do, how to do it, and what not to do.

Morals dictate reactions or impulses perceived as right or wrong and good or bad. Police officers and politicians must conform to the highest standards of ethical conduct with professional discretion to do what is right.

Misconduct by a few *Bad Apples* gives the Law Enforcement profession a lousy name, reflecting negatively on *Good Apples* (good police officers). Sympathetic police officials repeatedly excuse bad apples ignoring standards of moral conduct and straining budgets with costly lawsuits.

Personal beliefs, principles, or values must never afford — any law enforcement officer — the privilege to violate the Constitutional rights of any citizen, regardless of race, ethnicity, gender, status, or skin color.

First and foremost, let us agree that *Bad Apples* symbolize the *"Sad Truth"* about the institution of Law Enforcement in the United States of America. *Bad Apples* foster extremist views, exploit the rule of law, violate the civil rights of people of color, and abuse authority, disavowing 21st-century policing concepts and best practices.

In May 2020, considering violent protests across the country following the death of George Floyd at the hands of the city of Minneapolis police officers, the White House national security adviser Robert O'Brien spoke to TV host Jake Tapper on CNN's State of the Union.

Source:
CNN POLITICS / May 31, 2020
"National security adviser: 'I Don't Think There's Systemic Racism' in US Police Forces."
By Devan Cole and Sarah Westwood, CNN

> *"No, I don't think there's systemic racism. I think 99.9% of our law enforcement officers are great Americans. Many of them are African Americans, Hispanic, Asian, they're working the toughest neighborhood, they've got the hardest jobs to do in this country and I think they're amazing, great Americans," O'Brien told CNN's Jake Tapper on 'State of the Union' when asked if systemic racism was a problem for police agencies (Cole & Westwood, 2020). "There are some bad apples in there. And there -- some bad cops are racist. And some cops are -- maybe don't have the right training. And some are just bad cops. And they need to be rooted out because there are a few bad apples that are giving law enforcement a terrible name" (Cole & Westwood, 2020).*

I suggest there are no excuses for political appointees to *distort* or *"soft-pedal"* issues with incendiary or appeasing rhetoric. They should speak with truth and conviction, particularly knowing the volatile nature of a problematic national issue. The racial or political implications are too provocative. Moreover, distorting or *"tap dancing"* issues to appease audiences to gain political favor undermines the democratic principles and values of our great nation.

We regard *"Good Apples"* as exceptional police officers serving and protecting citizens and communities with trust, integrity, and respect. They command courage, self-control, knowledge of laws, and ethical standards.

Source:
DALLAS MORNING NEWS EDITORIAL / JUNE 03, 2020
"Are 'Bad Apples' the Problem, or Is Policing Across the Country in Need of Overhaul"

>*"Hard problems require tough solutions, and in the case of decades of tension between minority communities and police departments, the remedy requires all of us to acknowledge that the problem is more pervasive than the transgressions of a few bad apples" (Dallas Morning News Editorial, 2020).*

>*"Just to be clear, police officers have one of the toughest jobs, and those who do their jobs with respect and dignity deserve our esteem and support for their dedication to public service" (Dallas Morning News Editorial, 2020).*

Sheriff and police departments must identify misguided officers who serve -- *as human wolves cloaked as sheep* -- denying fair treatment and equal justice for marginalized citizens. They demonstrate white supremacy views without shame or guilt. I speak candidly without hesitation to denounce racist behavior that can ruin good police officers, too.

Source:
ROLLING STONE MAGAZINE / May 12, 2021
"The Enemy Within: Race and White Supremacy in American Policing"
By Steve Volk

> "Accusations of racism, and white supremacy, conjure visions of extremists – hateful men in white hoods or wearing swastikas, bent on murder. But merely covering up for racism, tolerating it, disregarding it – those are also racist acts. Such a summation sweeps up any union boss, rank-and-file officer, police chief, or politician who brushes over racism" (Volk, 2021).

Sheriffs and police chiefs must commit to a clear mission to build public trust, establish relationships, promote best practices, and closely monitor internal controls. They must move in the right direction with proficient personnel to maintain quality operations.

Source:

BRENNAN CENTER FOR JUSTICE / August 27, 2020
"Hidden in Plain Sight: Racism, White Supremacy, and Far-Right Militancy in Law Enforcement"
By Michael German

> *"The most effective way for law enforcement agencies to restore public trust and prevent racism from influencing law enforcement actions is to prohibit individuals who are members of white supremacist groups or who have a history of explicitly racist conduct from becoming law enforcement officers in the first place, or from remaining officers once bias is demonstrated" (German, 2020).*

I believe, too, that *We, the People,* must reevaluate how to appreciate *"Good Apples"* for their courage and commitment to do what is right for the right reasons. Public scrutiny and media reports are often unkind to good police officers, overshadowing positive deeds that surpass expectations and the call of duty.

The following provides interesting perspectives offered by veteran news reporters about the police officers viewed as *"Good Apples."* The reporters offer views that may vary – agency to agency -- depending on the executive leadership and mid-level management culture.

Sergeants and lieutenants are key to sustaining top performing agencies. Depending on the leadership, culture, size, and budget resources, some agencies' administrative and operational practices are more prudent than others.

Organizational leadership and culture directly impact employee performance and efficiency. Police officers precisely know the laws, policies, rules, and expectations and what they can get away with. They know, too, the supervisors or commanders who will overlook or misrepresent misconduct complaints and who will not. Disciplinary violations will increase if the leadership or culture allows officers to not follow or monitor general policies and procedures correctly. *Bad Apples* will logically increase, too.

Firm supervision with a fair disciplinary process must send a clear, believable message to Bad Apples. Once police leadership and culture are intolerant of Bad Apples, the disciplinary cases will decrease. Trust, cooperation, and certainty with the disciplinary process should improve, too. Research studies suggest that leadership and culture can help or hurt the morale of any department's rank and file.

On April 24, 2021, A.J. Kaufman, ALPHA NEWS, wrote, *"Most Police Are Good Apples: It's easy for wealthy celebrities and protected politicians to bash cops, but maybe someday they'll admit they'd never last an hour doing what these brave men and women do every day"* (Kaufman, 2021).

On June 9, 2020, Larry Levine, editor and publisher, of THE POLITICAL DISH, wrote an article entitled, *"Only the Good Apples in Police Departments Can Bring About Real Change."* An excerpt from the article provided an explanation that attracted my attention.

"No one knows who the 'bad apples' are in a police department better than the 'good apples.' But it's a tall order to ask any police officer to swim against the culture of law enforcement. The infamous 'thin blue line' in every police department demands loyalty and silence and punishes even perceived disloyalty. An officer who reports or interferes with the bad behavior of a fellow officer will be scorned, shunned, hazed, harassed, and maybe even killed 'in the line of duty' by a gun that never is found. The 'thin blue line' was created by bad cops to protect bad cops and woe to the good cop who dares cross it" (Levine, 2020).

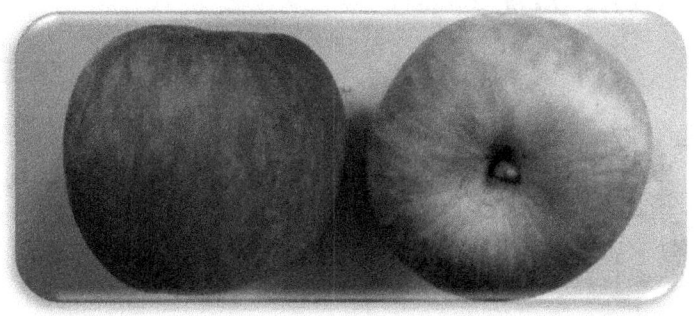

"Bad Apples"

Source:
PATRICIA ROBERTS-MILLER / June 12, 2020
*"Bad Apples, Police Brutality, Reform"*By
Patricia Roberts-Miller

> *"People are using 'it's a few bad apples' to say that we shouldn't try to make major changes to policing, but a few minor reforms at best. And I do not understand why people say that"* (Roberts-Miller, 2020).

> *"The saying is not, 'A few bad apples give the other apples a bad reputation,' or 'A few bad apples' shouldn't be used to think about the bunch as a whole"* (Roberts-Miller, 2020).

> *"The saying is, 'A few bad apples ruin the whole bunch.' The metaphor means that once one apple starts to rot, it starts a process that will quickly rot all the apples. If that rotten apple has been there a while, the whole bunch is rotten. Putting a rotten apple on suspension does not make it any less rotten"*
> *(Roberts-Miller, 2020).*

Source:
COURIER / June 16, 2020
"The 'Warrior Mindset' of Cops Is One of the Biggest Obstacles to Police Reform."
By Keya Vakil

> *"You cannot complain about a few bad apples when you grow the trees,"* said Lacy Lew Nguyen Wright,

an associate director at BLD PWR, a nonprofit that seeks to fight systemic oppression. "We have created a system that has repeatedly told police officers that they will be protected in these situations, that they can get away with this behavior, and when you tell people that it is allowed, you cannot then be shocked that people will then stoop to this level of behavior" (Vikal, 2020).

Lacy is the Executive Director of the Hillman Grad Foundation, overseeing its Mentorship Lab and Rising Voices initiative with Indeed. #BLDPWR (Build Power) engages with athletes & entertainers to use their platform to advance radical social change & dismantle systemic oppression (Vikal, 2020).

2 *Audacity of Hypocrisy*

Can you believe it? Racial hypocrisy in American Democracy and Law Enforcement started somewhere and somehow. Historical data suggest that devastating events besieging the early days of Slavery and the Civil War era are responsible.

How dare We, the People, believe that the -- God-fearing, Flag-waving, Patriotic -- Founding Fathers who penned the original Declaration of Independence and U.S. Constitution viewed *freedom, liberty, equality, inalienable rights,* and the *pursuit of happiness* as applicable to all Americans. My -- public school -- American History teachers taught me that those original documents qualified all citizens for *freedom, liberty,* and *equality.* If that is so, what happened to the evidential proof over the years?

Let us consider three devout values, *freedom, liberty,* and *equality,* promised as moral well-being and opportunity in our democratic society. Strangely, the Founding Fathers omitted any reference to human dignity, civil rights, or civil liberties for Black people. They consciously spoke and inscribed one thing, then immorally embraced Slavery as another.

Source:
HYPERALLERGIC / June 18, 2020
"Historical Painting Is Altered to Show Most Declaration of Independence Signatories Were Enslavers"
By Valentina Di Liscia

> *"John Trumbull's painting 'Declaration of Independence,' which hangs in the rotunda of the US Capitol, commemorates the document that freed the United States, formerly the 13 British colonies, from European rule in 1776. The concept of freedom, though, was severely limited: slavery was only abolished nearly a century later, and its reverberations of racist violence and mass incarceration subjugate Black people to this day"* (Di Liscia, 2020).
>
> *"In a poignant illustration of this hypocrisy, Arlen Parsa, a Chicago-based documentary filmmaker,*

covered the faces of every enslaver in the painting with a red circle: a 34 out of the 47 men pictured, <u>most of whom</u> were signers of the Declaration. (The fact-checking website PolitiFact has <u>corroborated</u> Parsa's count" (Di Liscia, 2020).

"Declaration of Independence" Founding Fathers, 1818

Source:
BETTER GOVERNMENT ASSOCIATION/September 10, 2019
"Fact Check: Evidence Shows Most of the Men in Famous 'Declaration of Independence' Painting Were Slaveholders"
By Tom Kertscher

"Here are the 34 men in the painting found to be slaveholders, in alphabetical order by last name: Josiah Bartlett, Charles Carroll, Samuel Chase, Abraham Clark, George Clinton, John Dickinson, William Floyd, Benjamin Franklin, John Hancock, Benjamin Harrison, Joseph Hewes, Thomas Heyward Jr., William Hooper, Stephen Hopkins, Francis Hopkinson, Thomas Jefferson, Richard Henry Lee. And Francis Lewis, Philip Livingston, Robert R. Livingston, Thomas Lynch, Arthur Middleton, Lewis Morris, Robert Morris, William Paca, George Read, Benjamin Rush, Edward Rutledge, Richard Stockton, William Whipple, Thomas Willing, John Witherspoon, Oliver Wolcott, and George Wythe" (Kertscher, 2019).

"The men who did not own slaves also tended to be well-to-do. Here are the 13 who apparently did not own slaves: John Adams, Samuel Adams, George Clymer, William Ellery, Elbridge Gerry, Samuel Huntington, Thomas McKean, Robert Treat Paine, Roger Sherman, Charles Thomson, George Walton, William Williams, and James Willson" (Kertscher, 2019).

Enslaved Black people endured hell from the slaveholders. I imagine the physical and emotional atrocities perpetrated were unthinkable to bear. Black people were counted as *three-fifths of a person* to fulfill State representation in the U.S. Congress. They were stripped of their human dignity with no freedom or rights that White people were bound to respect.

Source:
THOUGHTCO - HUMANITIES, ISSUES / October 30, 2020
"The History of the Three-Fifths Compromise"
By Nadra Kareem Nittle

> "First introduced by James Wilson and Roger Sherman on June 11, 1787, the three-fifths compromise counted enslaved people as three-fifths of a person. This agreement meant that the Southern states got more electoral votes than if the enslaved population had not been counted at all, but fewer votes than if the enslaved population had been fully counted" (Nittle, 2020).

Enslaved Black people overcame the abomination of slavery with the ultimate sacrifice by the *Grace, Goodness,* and *Mercy* of the Almighty GOD. They existed as an inferior and subhuman race of people. Today, in the minds of many, that exact racist perception still lurks to subvert American Democracy and Law Enforcement. Black people have come a long way; there remains a long way.

I am reminded of a religious perspective that describes the hypocritical enslavers. Proverbs 23:7 says, *"For as he thinketh in his heart, so is he: Eat and drink, saith he to thee; but his heart is not with thee."* (KJV)

The Founding Fathers wrote and affirmed one common adage with their quills and mouths, *"All men are created equal."* On the contrary, in their hearts, they denied Black people fundamental human rights, championing something different: *human bondage.*

Which can we believe? I suggest that we think of their hearts. Because their hypocritical thinking and beliefs depicted the reality of who they were. Their core beliefs and values reflected shallow thinking, readily exposing hypocrisy and self-righteousness.

The question arises: *"Why did the two original national documents declare that All Men Are Created Equal?"* I argue that the Founding Fathers' phrasing of *"created equal"* depicted typical hypocrisy with a disingenuous assertion, then and now. Undoubtedly, their sinful oppression relished the convenience of *free labor* over the misery and pain of human suffering.

When someone or something is "overlooked" or "looked over," there is a fundamental reason. It is logical to assume the omission was an oversight, a mistake, or an error. Intent may or may not factor into the reason(s) for the deletion. Whatever the case, the white founding fathers and landowners consciously disavowed human rights and dignity for enslaved Black people.

With a Shepherd's heart, Pastor Robert J. Matthews

In December 2022, I listened as my pastor, ROBERT J. MATTHEWS, contrasted two terms, *"overlooked"* and *"looked over,"* in a Sunday sermon at New Hope Baptist Church of Memphis, 2356 Elvis Presley Blvd, Memphis, TN 38106. Pastor Matthews convincingly explained that when somebody or something is *looked over,* you *"knew they were there"* or *"knew it was there."*

Comparably, the term *overlooked* denotes the opposite; you *"were unaware"* that somebody or something was there. There is a distinct difference.

For my purpose, I contend that the Founding Fathers were ruthless enslavers who knew that Black people were there. However, they chose to *look over* the dehumanizing bondage and maltreatment suffered by the enslaved people.

Source:
COMMENTARY MAGAZINE – LAW, GOVERNMENT & SOCIETY / May 1987

"Why Blacks, Women & Jews Are Not Mentioned in the Constitution"

By Robert A. Goldwin

> "As Benjamin Hooks, executive director of the National Association for the Advancement of Colored People, put it in criticism of the original Constitution: 'Article I, section 2, clause 3 of the Constitution starts off with a quota: three-fifths. That is what Black folks were in that original Constitution.' Hooks is not alone in this view. The historian John Hope Franklin has written of this same clause that the Founders 'degraded the human spirit by equating five black men with three white men'; and the constitutional-law professor Lino Graglia contends that the provision 'that a slave was to be counted as three-fifths of a free person for purposes of representation' shows 'how little the Constitution had to do with aspirations for brotherhood or human dignity'" (Goldwin, 1987).

Source:
BERKELEY PUBLIC POLICY JOURNAL / November 12, 2020
"The Dangers of Teaching American Exceptionalism"
By Vinay A. Ramesh

> *"American ideals didn't include equality for women who fought for suffrage and only attained the right to vote in 1920. It didn't include equality for Native Americans, whose land this country stole, displacing millions. It didn't include equality for Black people who are STILL fighting to this day to be recognized as equals. Equal protection may have been granted in name, but this country is still far from universally accepting Black people and people of color as equal in their eyes and hearts" (Ramesh, 2020).*

HENRY LOUIS GATES, JR., one of America's most accomplished literary critics, teachers, filmmakers, and historians, authored an intriguing article about Abraham Lincoln, the 16th president of the United States of America. As of this writing, Professor Gates is the Alphonse Fletcher University Professor and Director of the Hutchins Center for African and African American Research at Harvard University.

I found Professor Gates' article: "*Was Lincoln a Racist?*" quite attractive and eye-opening for a Lincoln buff like me and, perhaps, many others. The article, published on February 12, 2009, describes Lincoln's candor and intuition about *Negroes, Slavery,* and *White Supremacy.* I highly recommend reading Professor Gate's entire article. I was struck by an 1858 speech Lincoln delivered in Charleston, Illinois.

Regarding Snopes: Fact Check at www.snopes.com, Lincoln made "authentic" remarks, on September 18, 1858, at Charleston, Illinois, that have attracted *"renewed attention."* The remarks *"came at the beginning of his opening speech at the fourth of seven famous debates with Stephen Douglas, during Lincoln's unsuccessful campaign for the U.S. Senate in Illinois. Lincoln had been under attack from Democrats who accused him of supporting racial equality, and his comments were a defense against those allegations."*

President Abraham Lincoln, 1858

Other Black people, too, undoubtedly lauded President Lincoln's conflicted aspiration to abolish human enslavement to unify the United States for the right reasons. Professor Gates points out the introspective conflicts Lincoln grappled with about race and slavery during his presidency.

Like others, I grew up believing and living Black history that President Lincoln was a hero to Black people in America. The following are enlightening excerpts from Professor Gates's informative public news article.

Source:
THE ROOT / February 09, 2009
"Was Lincoln a Racist?"
By Henry Louis Gates Jr.

"But my engagement with the great leader turned to confusion when I was a senior in high school. I stumbled upon an essay that Lerone Bennett Jr. published in Ebony *magazine entitled 'Was Abe Lincoln a White Supremacist?' A year later, as an undergraduate at Yale, I read an even more troubling essay that W.E.B. DuBois had published in* The Crisis *magazine in May 1922. DuBois wrote that Lincoln was one huge jumble of contradictions: 'he was big enough to be inconsistent—cruel, merciful; peace-loving, a fighter; despising Negroes and letting them fight and vote; protecting slavery and freeing slaves.' He was a man—a big, inconsistent, brave man'"* (Gates, 2009).

"So many hurt and angry readers flooded DuBois' mailbox that he wrote a second essay in the next issue of the magazine, in which he defended his position this way: 'I love him not because he was perfect but because he was not and yet triumphed' .... To prove his point, Du Bois included this quote from a speech Lincoln delivered in 1858 in Charleston, Illinois" (Gates, 2009).

"I will say, then, that I am not, nor ever have been, in favor of bringing about in any way the social and political equality of the white and black races—that I

am not, nor ever have been, in favor of making voters or jurors of Negroes, nor of qualifying them to hold office, nor to intermarry with white people; and I will say in addition to this, that there is a physical difference between the white and black races which I believe will forever forbid the two races living together on terms of social and political equality. And inasmuch as they cannot so live, while they do remain together there must be the position of superior and inferior, and I, as much as any other man, am in favor of having the superior position assigned to the white race." – Abraham Lincoln

Meanwhile, nationwide news reports and video evidence convinced me that *White Supremacy* and *White Privilege* remain twin bedrocks undermining racial justice. Extremist beliefs and values should never suppress human rights with hypocrisy and hate. Meaningful reforms are inevitable for a brighter future in Democracy and Law Enforcement.

First and foremost, we must face the truth about our problems and differences with agreeable solutions. The rule of law, respect, and racial decency must prevail for the greater prosperity of Democracy. *We, the People,* must accept no less.

A 46-year law enforcement career qualified me to encourage others with unbiased insight. It took me that long to fully comprehend the negative influence of racial hypocrisy and hate in a broken policing culture. I operated in denial with blind loyalty and a false sense of trust. Because of blind patriotism and brainwashing, I failed to see the forest for the trees, too. However, my career experiences and parental wisdom taught me how to become an independent thinker.

Eventually, I awakened to realize how the same broken policing culture had victimized me – a police officer -- because of my skin color. After that, I never succumbed to a subservient mentality to follow other police officers when I knew they were wrong.

Lil Mama always reminded me, *"Boy, the truth will set you free – trust GOD."* Another piece of *Granddaddy's* wisdom that I cashed in on, *"Nobody can ride on your back unless you bend your butt over and let them get on there."* His favorite ending, *"Do you understand me?"* I answered quickly, *"Yes, sir."*

Today, the reckless indiscretion baffles me, as demonstrated by misguided officers in deadly shootings during traffic stops involving unarmed Black victims. I suggest sheriffs and police chiefs move judiciously to address alarming decision-making patterns, reviewing practices and increasing *Implicit Bias* and *De-escalation* training.

My career experiences and challenges resulted in meaningful lessons learned: *What to do, how to do it,* and *what not to do.* My partners and I tackled dangerous situations that required patience and thoughtful strategies for reasonable outcomes. However, we remained alert for elements of surprise. We did what we had to do for safe resolutions.

We were prepared to *articulate* and *justify* our responses as required. I learned to document details, sticking to the facts – not lies or distortions. On the other hand, I realized that John Q. Public often misunderstands the *"realities of policing,"* particularly citizens who rush to judgment with false assumptions or misplaced emotions about police officers. Conversely, the exact realization can apply to police officers, too.

Above all, I never adopted the *"Us vs. Them"* or *"Warrior"* policing mentality and never abused any citizen because of race, ethnicity, gender, or skin color. I speak with the weapon of truth, unabashed by what others think, even though it might sound like hogwash to those comfortable denying or misrepresenting the truth.

3 *Believe It, or Not*

"*American Democracy*" refers to a democratic government formed of, for, and by "*We, the People*" to pursue freedom, liberty, and justice for all. Representative Democracy, ruled by the people, fails without the rule of law and the protective services of police officers to maintain public order and safe communities. Police officers are an absolute necessity.

However, police officers and politicians threaten Democracy whenever they, explicitly or implicitly, disregard any American citizen's constitutional rights and liberties with racial bias or abusive practices. This dilemma leads to the question, "*What is the role of police officers in our Democracy?*"

I view police officers as *guardians* of Democracy and justice, preserving life and property, keeping the peace, and enforcing the rule of law with truth, courage, and integrity. They swear by an oath to serve and protect all citizens regardless of race, ethnicity, or skin color.

Because police officers possess the authority and responsibility of enforcing the rule of law, they must maintain a higher moral or ethical standard than citizens. It is beyond my comprehension that *sworn* police officers deliberately defy Democracy with the shame of racial bias and hate.

The social and political realities of modern times demanding justice for all citizens continue to expose the blissful ignorance of white supremacy. According to FBI and Anti-Defamation League reports, right-wing extremists are increasingly infiltrating the ranks of police departments and government entities across the country.

Police leaders and politicians must address systemic racism, and its root causes with honesty and transparency to preclude hypocrisy. In other words, be honest in disavowing racial bias and extremism. America needs a new direction to restore moral trust and prominence in Democracy and Law Enforcement.

I found the Law Enforcement profession incredibly challenging during my career. However, I have no regrets or second thoughts about becoming a police officer. Nonetheless, it was clear that the abusive attitudes and behavior of misguided white police officers normalized a broken policing culture, threatening the quality of life for Black people.

As a Memphis Police rookie, I often heard white coworkers make subtle implications that *"Black people were inferior to White people."* The implications really *"burned my craw."* I could not believe it. They brazenly said that in my presence. However, I smartly dismissed it to learn my job effectively. I grew to gain much respect for the good white coworkers who helped me perform my duties and responsibilities.

Today, sheriffs, police chiefs, administrators, and subordinates must step up to the plate and conform to 21st-century policing precepts and best practices. Perhaps, fixing or reforming a broken policing culture is the most difficult leadership challenge they will experience. Too many consciously resist beneficial change due to inherent bias or the unwillingness to divorce old ways.

My beliefs and opinions were impacted by what I saw of white police officers as a little boy and teenager, plus my challenges as a Black Memphis police officer and Shelby County deputy sheriff. In other words, *"What I saw, what I experienced, and how I felt influenced me."*

Consequently, with extremists increasingly infiltrating Law Enforcement agencies, sympathetic sheriffs, police chiefs, and union officials repeatedly deny the truth. Many police officials continue to ignore misconduct complaints filed by citizens. They feel obligated to defend rebellious, overly zealous subordinates in denial of the misconduct allegations and indisputable evidence.

Today, police misconduct or wrongdoing appears more legitimately contested in courts of law than in past years. Lawyers are winning more high-profile criminal and civil cases against police officers than ever before. Sadly, more officers are indicted for crimes and civil rights violations against minority citizens.

Source:
BRENNAN CENTER FOR JUSTICE / August 27, 2020
"Hidden in Plain Sight: Racism, White Supremacy, and Far-Right Militancy in Law Enforcement"
By Michael German

> *"In 2017, the FBI reported that white supremacists posed a "persistent threat of lethal violence" that has produced more fatalities than any other category of domestic terrorists since 2000. Alarmingly, internal FBI policy documents have also warned agents assigned to domestic terrorism cases that the white supremacist and anti-government militia groups they investigate often have "active links" to law enforcement officials. The harms that armed law enforcement officers affiliated with violent white supremacist and anti-government militia groups can*

inflict on American society could hardly be overstated" (German, 2020).

Conspiring against Democracy under the pretense of patriotism and freedom of speech appears legitimate for white supremacy conspirators. However, I am confident that American Democracy remains resilient despite the increasingly hate-spewed rhetoric by right-wingers and conspiracy theorists.

America, a leader in Democracy, was built on the backs of enslaved Black people. All people are created equal in the sight of GOD, regardless of race, ethnicity, gender, status, or skin color. I challenge radicalized police officers to redeem their *"hearts and souls morally"* and realize that GOD is omnipotent and still in charge. We all must account for sins and transgressions against our fellow men.

Right-wing extremists propagate fears and false assumptions about the increase in violent crimes, blaming people of color. Nevertheless, in Tennessee and abroad, stubborn right-wing legislators will not support common sense gun safety legislation to curb gun violence. It is mindboggling. Sensible gun safety laws requiring responsible gun ownership must be a priority. Gun access and violent crime are out of control in America.

I coined a new phrase, *"Intellectual Treason,"* to describe the resistance of lawmakers who neglect to endorse common sense gun safety legislation. They conveniently ignore the will of the people protesting the senseless killings of innocent men, women, and children from increased gun violence nationwide. The heedless legislators choose to uphold partisan politics supporting gun manufacturers and extremism at any cost. They know better but fail to do better.

On August 5, 2019, James P. Steyer, founder and CEO of COMMON SENSE MEDIA, issued an enlightening statement in an online article *"Gun Control Laws Are Common Sense."*

"There is no place for violence in our country, in our communities, and online. It's critical that Congress acts immediately to ensure that our country has responsible gun laws, so the nation doesn't have to wake up to the horror of yet another mass shooting" (Steyer, 2019).

"A lack of sensible gun reform laws combined with escalating hate and extremism puts our country at a point of crisis. Immigrants and communities of color are being unfairly targeted, and kids and families don't feel safe, online or in their communities" (Steyer, 2019).

On October 4, 2022, Nick Wilson, CENTER FOR AMERICAN PROGRESS, author of the article *"Fact Sheet:*

Weakening Requirements to Carry a Concealed Firearm Increases Violent Crime," wrote the following:

> "Right-to-carry laws increase violent crime, firearm robberies, gun thefts, workplace homicides, and mass shootings by making it easier for almost anyone to carry a concealed handgun in public. Conservative state legislatures weakening requirements to carry a concealed firearm is a recent trend that makes policing more difficult and dangerous, resulting in law enforcement leaders across the country publicly opposing these laws. Scientific research consistently shows that the removal of concealed carry permitting systems is associated with higher rates of gun homicides and violent crime" (Wilson, 2022).

The following references a Congressional Gold Medal ceremony honoring U.S. Capitol police officers and police departments that defended the massive assault on the U.S. Capitol building on January 6, 2021. The ceremony exposed the audacious hypocrisy demonstrated by GOP congressional members. Consequently, GOP members should be more sensible in publicly honoring the insurrectionists who stormed the U.S. Capitol.

On December 5, 2022, the gold medal ceremony recognized 140 police officers, assisting police departments, and the family members representing five officers deceased due to the violent Capitol attack.

A shameful, dark reflection of the ceremony occurred when several family members refused to shake the hand of two GOP congressional leaders while receiving a gold medal on behalf of their fallen loved one. Family members snubbed the two GOP leaders for failing to acknowledge the truth following the Capitol attack.

Source:
CBS NEWS / December 6, 2022
"Family of fallen Capitol Police officer refuses to shake hands with McCarthy, McConnell at medal ceremony."
By Scott MacFarlane

> *"The family of Capitol Police Officer Brian Sicknick — his mother, father and brother — refused to shake hands with Senate Minority Leader Mitch McConnell and House Republican Leader Kevin McCarthy at a Congressional Gold Medal ceremony honoring the police departments that worked to save the U.S. Capitol during the <u>riot on Jan. 6, 2021</u>"* (MacFarlane, 2022).

"We honor their service and sacrifice in answering the call to defend Democracy in one of our darkest hours," said House Speaker Nancy Pelosi.

His brother Ken Sicknick told CBS News that Republican leaders *"have no idea what integrity is" (MacFarlane, 2022).*

Sicknick referred to Rep. Louis Gohmert (R-Texas), who presented an American Flag flown over the U.S. Capitol to a Jan. 6 rioter and told them they were patriots. *"It's disgusting. Takes away everything my brother's done. Takes away the heroism my brother showed." "For Republicans,"* he said, *"It's party first" (MacFarlane, 2022).*

"... We must all learn to live together as brothers, or we will all perish together as fools. We are tied together in the single garment of destiny, caught in an inescapable network of mutuality. And whatever affects one directly, affects all indirectly. For some strange reason I can never be what I ought to be until you are what you ought to be, and you can never be what you ought to be until I am what I ought to be. This is the way God's universe is made; this is the way it is structured ..."

-- Dr. Martin Luther King, Jr.

4 Policing Culture

Today, it is a cultural shame that white supremacy ideology influences American Democracy and Law Enforcement, requiring urgent attention in a multiracial society of free-thinking people. According to an article entitled *"Prevalence of white supremacists in law enforcement demands drastic change,"* by Hassan Kanu, REUTERS NEWS AGENCY, published May 12, 2022, a May 6 investigation supported my assertion.

The Reuter's investigation revealed: *"More and more, the evidence suggests the 'white supremacist infiltration of law enforcement' that the FBI warned about back in 2006 is getting worse. And it points to a desperate need for policies – departmental and legislative – to prohibit people who engage in racist conduct or join white supremacist groups from becoming police officers or remaining on the force"* (Kanu, 2022).

Source:
PENNSYLVANIA CAPITAL-STAR / March 12, 2023
"Policing has its roots in slave catching. To change it, we must change that legacy" / Opinion.
By Terrence A. Alladin, Lebanon Valley College

> *"Police culture is founded on racial inequity. The earliest known police in America, the slave patrols, were established on a foundation of racism. Those 19th century officers were used to carry out the will of both the plantation owners and the state and keep Black slaves under control. Racism in contemporary policing can be traced from this early policing group to the Jim Crow era, through Civil Rights, and to present-day mass incarceration" (Alladin, 2023).*

Source:
THE CONVERSATION / Updated June 02, 2020
"The racist roots of American policing: From slave patrols to traffic stops." By Connie Hassett-Walker, Norwich University

> *"Policing's institutional racism of decades and centuries ago still matters because policing culture has not changed as much as it could. For many African Americans, law enforcement represents a <u>legacy of reinforced inequality</u> in the justice system and*

resistance to advancement – even under pressure from the civil rights movement and its legacy" (Hassett-Walker, 2020).

Far from perfect, I commend the Shelby County Sheriff's Office and other Greater Memphis law enforcement agencies that achieved CALEA accreditation for excellence in organization and service. CALEA is an acronym for *The Commission on Accreditation for Law Enforcement Agencies, Inc.* This accomplishment is well-deserved for the citizens of Memphis and Shelby County, Tennessee.

Source:
COURIER / June 16, 2020
"The 'Warrior Mindset' of Cops Is One of the Biggest Obstacles to Police Reform." By Keya Vakil

> *"For decades, many Americans have viewed police officers as the unequivocal 'good guys,' and police officers have, in turn, internalized that perception. They have embraced the mantra of the 'thin blue line,' which cops use to assert that they are the only thing that prevents society from descending into violent chaos" (Vakil, 2020).*

Nevertheless, Law Enforcement agencies sustaining discriminatory practices and misconduct patterns must improve. I highly recommend a *"National Standardized Policy"* to govern a broken policing culture nationwide. National news accounts continually sensationalize the deadly shootings of unarmed Black victims and tactical indiscretions by misguided police officers during traffic stops and public encounters.

Source:
PEW Research Center / June 3, 2020
"10 Things We Know About Race and Policing in the U.S."
By Drew DeSilver, Michael Lipka, and Dalia Fahmy

> *"Majorities of both black and white Americans say black people are treated less fairly than whites in dealing with the police and by the criminal justice system as a whole. In a 2019 Center survey, 84% of black adults said that, in dealing with police, blacks are generally treated less fairly than whites; 63% of whites said the same. Similarly, 87% of blacks and 61% of whites said the U.S. criminal justice system treats black people less fairly"* (DeSilver, Lipka, Fahmy, 2020).

Underserved communities yearn for meaningful collaboration between police leaders, politicians, clergy members, and concerned citizens to address high crime and lawlessness. Meaningful collaboration means genuine participation from police agencies, government entities, churches, and community stakeholders. The safety and welfare of marginalized communities should not be *"looked over"* or taken for granted.

Sadly, right-wing legislators, state and congressional, have ignored requests from sheriffs, police chiefs, and law-abiding citizens for sensible gun safety legislation to curb gun violence. The right-wing legislators appear indifferent to considering commonsense gun laws to control gun violence and senseless killings in America.

Source:
ABUSEOFPOWER.INFO / 2002
"Police Culture" By Diane Wetendorf

> *"There are two sides to the police culture: formal and informal. The formal side consists of policies and procedures that dictate what officers are supposed to do. They are required to enforce the law in a way that abides by the U.S. Constitution, which guarantees people equal protection of the law: The law discriminates against no one, and no one is above the law" (Wetendorf, 2002).*
>
> *"The informal side of the police culture consists of the attitudes, beliefs, and values that determine how*

officers behave and what they actually do in their day-to-day practices" (Wetendorf, 2002).

Law Enforcement officers, too, deserve recognition for meritorious service as earned. They, too often, receive unwarranted public scrutiny for their spontaneous reactions to inevitable outcomes. Unfortunately, they are *"lambasted"* if they do and *"lambasted"* if not. In other words, *"caught between a rock and hard place."* What a job!

Source:
POLICE1.com / October 7, 2020
"You Can't Legislate Culture - Here's How to Really Implement Change" By Barry A. Reynolds

> *"Policies don't drive behavior, culture does. You can develop all the policies (or legislation) you want, but if the culture of the organization is not in line with the terminal values of the profession and the highest organizational expectations, your policies are worth little more than a campaign promise"* (Reynolds, 2020).

> *"Leadership systems that become complacent in addressing problems, look the other way when bad things happen, or keep officers that have no business*

remaining in this profession undermine their own agencies by poisoning the culture" (Reynolds, 2020).

I enrolled at the Memphis Police Academy in March 1968 and at Shelby County Sheriff's Academy in August 1985. Respectively, after graduation, Uniform Patrol Division training officers pushed identical shortsighted standard practices at both agencies: *"Forget what you learned in that 'damn' Academy; we got you now."*

The veteran training officers insisted they could teach rookies *"better"* how to do the job correctly – not the Academy instructors. Unfortunately, new officers likely faced similar policing and training subcultures at Sheriff's Offices and Police Departments nationwide.

Source:
FBI LAW ENFORCEMENT BULLETIN / October 01, 2011
"Rethinking Ethics in Law Enforcement"
By Brian D. Fitch, Ph.D.

> *"Most officers enter law enforcement with minimal experience in the field or in handling the moral dilemmas that officers typically encounter. They learn how to perform their jobs, as well as recognize the organizational norms, values, and culture, from their peers and supervisors. While supervisors provide*

> *direct, formal reinforcement, officers' peers offer friendship and informal rewards that, in many cases, hold greater influence than official recognition from the agency. Also, police often spend considerable time socializing with other officers, both on and off the job. This sense of community drives officers to adopt the behaviors, values, and attitudes of the group to gain acceptance"* (Fitch, 2011).

Before 1972, the Memphis Police Department nor Shelby County Sheriff's Office followed a designated Field Training Officer (FTO) model. Both agencies eventually approved the San Jose Field Training Officer Model for training and evaluating new patrol officers.

According to the *Police Executive Research Forum (PERF)*, the San Jose Police Department's model became a mainstay in police training. Approximately 4,000 agencies use it.

Before the San Jose model, misguided trainers commonly influenced trainees with implicit biases and unethical practices targeting Black citizens. Misguided trainers rated trainees harshly when viewing them unsuitable for the job. Notably, the harsh ratings affected Black trainees more than others. However, all white training officers did not share this biased mindset or partake in the *"racial nonsense."*

During in-car conversations, objective discussions regarding racial or political issues were *"few and far between."* In many instances, I regarded most veteran trainers' racial and political views as slanted and obnoxious. Their views and opinions reminded me of my *Granddaddy's* wisdom, *"Empty wagons make a lot of noise."*

Field training assignments conveniently allowed misguided training officers to indoctrinate trainees with *"Us vs. Them"* or *"Warrior"* mentalities. Many found it pleasing to disparage marginalized citizens and communities. Helplessly, I witnessed *"rotten"* attitudes and behaviors go unchecked, seeding *Bad Apples.* Those officers likely convinced others to adopt unbecoming attitudes and behavior. Nevertheless, I tolerated the nonsense and completed my training probation as required.

Despite contrasting views and opinions on racial issues, my White partners and I understood the importance of sharing a common bond for safety's sake. Our lives depended on it. We all wanted to return home safely after each duty shift. Whenever any officer or deputy radioed for *"Help"* or *"Backup Assistance,"* fellow officers expedited in full force.

Black trainees occasionally complained of unfair performance assessments causing them to quit voluntarily or face termination. The supervisory or training opinions mainly represented false assumptions, baseless lies, or rumors. Fortunately, like others, I dismissed the nonsense and stayed focused.

Source:
THE NEW YORK TIMES/Opinion/The Editorial Board/
November 13, 2022
"Extremists in Uniform Put the Nation at Risk"

> *"Coordinating the efforts of the nation's roughly 18,000 law enforcement agencies have been notoriously difficult. Federal standards or even guidelines about how to deal with extremism — in recruiting officers, disciplining existing ones or even sharing information — would go a long way toward harmonizing law enforcement's response" (New York Times, 2022).*

5 *Training Culture*

In March 1968, I was a *"happy camper"* starting Basic Recruit training at the Memphis Police Academy (MPD). I admired six Hamilton High School graduates hired by MPD before me. Another high school friend and I graduated together from the Academy. *"We Hamiltonians"* were well-represented in City and County law enforcement.

Thanks to Inspector E.C. Swann *(RIP)*, the Academy director, and staff, the structured training environment introduced me to a challenging policing culture, not knowing what experiences or lessons awaited me. I was an *"eager beaver,"* physically and mentally prepared for Police recruit training. Failure or quitting was not an option for me. My wife, parents, and two young kids depended on me.

Like other Black police recruits, I followed all general policies, classroom instructions, and training protocols to the letter. I was fully aware of the racial hypocrisy, bias, and mind games we faced as Black recruits.

Police Rookies Look Future In Eye

The 44 new policemen who were graduated from the Memphis Police Training Academy last night expressed strong confidence in their futures in law enforcement.

"There is no greater agency than law enforcement," said Denver T. Yarbrough, 24, of 1785 Tampa Cove. "I have something to give to my neighborhood, to my parents and to the City of Memphis."

Neither recent court decisions nor social problems nor cries of police brutality appeared to intimidate the young men.

"I have accepted this job myself, and I'm ready to live with whatever it brings," said officer Yarbrough.

The recruits — pressed, starched and cleancut—waited in the wings at Armour Center before receiving their badges from Mayor Henry Loeb.

Michael J. Dougherty, 21, of 95 East Gage, said he was not worried about the effect of Supreme Court decisions on arrests and convictions.

"Although the court leaves you wondering what to expect next, my first challenge was to get through the training course and learn my duties," he said.

Officer Dougherty said he feels there should be a "tougher gun law" because it's too easy for people to get guns and "there are too many people shooting at policemen."

Insp. E. C. Swann, police training director, said 48 recruits and their families. Fire and Police Director Frank Holloman said Memphis will rise to the challenge to reduce crime and restore respect for authority.

"Tonight we are a nation in mourning at the senseless, reasonless act of crime that has taken the life of Senator Robert F. Kennedy," he said.

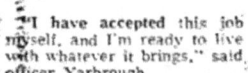 Denver T. Yarbrough

 Michael J. Dougherty

COMMERCIAL APPEAL / June 1968 / Memphis, TN

Subsequently, I stayed alert to minor details and quickly adapted to paying attention and taking nothing for granted. *"Attentiveness to detail"* became a positive trait of my DNA. Unbelievably, I enjoyed the training, respected others, and made many trainee mistakes. Consequently, by the grace of GOD, it was up to me to overcome the structural racial impediments and nonsense that temporarily stood in my way.

However, a subservient mentality, lack of self-esteem, or lack of decency were never a part of me and never will be. As a young Black parent, I anxiously conveyed the same to my kids and others I mentored or coached.

As a young Black man raised in South Memphis, the Memphis Police training experience was a new lease on my life with a fresh perspective on white police officers.

One day, I watched attentively and nervously as Inspector Swann dismissed two talkative white classmates from the Academy for outspoken negative opinions about Black people, sending a clear message to everybody. Both classmates were responding to a question directed to the class by Inspector Swann.

I quickly learned how to listen closely and keep my mouth shut. Listening is an art. *Lil Mama* always reminded me, *"Keep your 'trap' shut. Don't talk foolishly, trying to impress people. People will find out who you are and what you know in due time."*

The Memphis Police Academy provided a stimulating learning environment every moment I attended. Not one iota did I ever doubt my confidence. *Granddaddy's* and *Lil Mama's* religious faith, hard work, and wisdom prepared me for whatever. They never once insinuated or told me to play *"second fiddle"* or *"take a backseat"* to anybody.

Inspector Swann's no-nonsense leadership and sincere instructional approach left me in awe. Comparably, his compassion and objectivity led me to believe he was operating before his time, or perhaps, a new Memphis Police training culture was looming. His professionalism, wit, fairness, and ability to capture attention impressed me. He kept everybody alert and focused. It was *all business* and no playing around with him.

Nonetheless, I was naive to believe that this good white man's positive attributes mirrored the attitudes of the entire Memphis Police Department. Indeed, I was wrong. Racial tensions were high due to the *"1968 Sanitation Workers' Strike"* and Dr. Martin Luther King's assassination in Memphis.

While observing Inspector Swann and the Academy staff, I envisioned emulating their training techniques daydreaming that someday I would become a Law Enforcement instructor. Thank GOD; it came to fruition after I resigned from MPD in January 1984 and joined the Shelby County Sheriff's Office in August 1985.

Source:
TRAINING INDUSTRY / June 8, 2020
"Training Through the Decades: What Has Changed and What Has Not" By Jeff Seeley

> *"Although numerous changes have occurred over the last decade, what has not changed is the goal of training, which has always been, and always will be, to produce change in participants. How we achieve that goal looks a bit different today than it used to. Now, there is more emphasis on reinforcement and sustainment, and technologies have revolutionized the way participants perceive and engage with training. As we move deeper into the new decade, time will tell where the emphasis shifts and how training will continue to evolve"* (Seeley, 2020).

During the late 1960s and early 1970s, the in-service training culture in Memphis and Shelby County lacked interest and relevance. I am sure smaller towns and rural areas nearby were lacking in far more significant ways. However, In-service training improved tremendously as the years passed.

> *"To keep training relevant in a time of social distancing, most organizations operating within the training industry have been devising ways to offer virtual training programs. This shift to virtual as the primary medium for training delivery is, perhaps, the most significant change in the training industry over the last decade (possibly ever), and it was solidified in only a matter of months"* (Seeley, 2020).

I remember, circa 1971, City police officers and County deputy sheriffs frowned on attending in-service training classes. Most white officers felt that any police training about *Community Relations, Cultural Diversity,* or *Implicit Bias* was a joke and a waste of time.

However, some lousy attitudes changed when the *Tennessee P.O.S.T. Commission (Peace Officers Standards & Training)* approved a 5% pay supplement for 40 Hours of annual in-service training required for active, full-time law enforcement officers.

Later, the supplemental pay was adjusted to $600.00 for 40 Hours of in-service training each calendar year. Many veteran police officers still downplayed Community Relations concepts as irrelevant to policing.

During the summer of 1971, as a young patrolman, I attended a week of Memphis Police in-service training night sessions at the Claude Armour Fire & Police Training Center, 79 South Flicker Street. The interactive lectures occupied a spacious classroom for about 40 police officers. If an overflow existed, a room divider would open to adjoining rooms to accommodate more officers.

The disrespect for the guest instructors was pathetic. Officers were loud and boisterous, peppering the guest instructors with senseless questions and points of view, purposely wasting time. At the time, in-service training was new and unpopular for local city and county law enforcement officers.

On one occasion, I witnessed an Arkansas State University white female instructor stop and cry while lecturing at the podium. A group of obnoxious white officers harassed her terribly. They foolhardily challenged her subject matter and teaching points that did not meet their standards. It was not comfortable for the female instructor. Today, police agencies in Memphis and Shelby County refuse to tolerate any lousy behavior during in-service training classes.

Shelby County Sheriff's Office

Meanwhile, about six months after joining the Shelby County Sheriff's Office (SCSO) and being assigned to the Patrol Division, I met the Patrol Division's Executive Secretary, who coordinated training classes and prepared materials. She recognized me from a Memphis Amateur Boxing Association (MABA) event where the Sheriff's team participated. She was already familiar with my work in community relations and youth activities at the Memphis Police Department.

One day, at the old Sheriff's Shelby Oaks Substation, I stopped by the Secretary's office to speak as she prepared for an upcoming training class. She joked about how stressful the materials were to prepare. I told her I could share a Patrol Resource Manual to help her prepare better for the Patrol Procedures class.

The next day I delivered the manual. She was most appreciative. After reviewing it, the Secretary shared the information with the Training lieutenant, who advised the Chief of Patrol.

Surprisingly, while working the Patrol Baker Shift one evening, the Chief summoned me to his office. In the office, he advised me of an upcoming Reserve Officers training class. He wanted me to instruct a block of instruction on patrol procedures. He stared at me and said, *"You can do it. We know you got the experience and materials."* I proudly agreed to instruct the class.

The Chief emphasized to me not to worry about any ridicule from the veteran white officers. He said, *"I'll take care of that. You know how they are around here, right? If you don't, you'll learn."* He repeatedly reinforced that I do my job and he would take care of the rest.

The Chief stood up, moved away from his desk, shook my hand, and said jokingly, *"Now, get your damn butt out of here and start getting ready for that class."* I responded, *"Yes, sir, I appreciate it."* He was a hilarious chief with a heavy voice and strong sense of humor, well-liked among the rank and file. Thanks to him, I completed instructing the class; the rest is history.

I was grateful, stunned, and could not believe the opportunity happened for me to show what I could do. It surprised me because I was a Black deputy sheriff – a new kid on the block -- with 16 years of Memphis PD experience. I heard bickering among other officers, some asked, *"What the hell is Yarbrough trying to do, kiss the Sheriff's butt?"* However, no way I would be intimidated to turn down the opportunity.

Several days later, the Baker Shift's lieutenant called me into his office. I closed the door. He said, *"I understand you'll be teaching a Reserve patrol class."* I responded, *"Yes, sir, the Chief asked me to do it."* The lieutenant replied, *"If you want to stand up in front of those' f---kers,' that's up to you!"* He quickly stopped, gathered his thoughts and tone, and said, *"I'm sorry; I didn't mean to say that."* He changed the subject at that point. I immediately thought, *"Oh, yea, you meant it."*

Perhaps, his remark indicated how others like him felt about me and the training class. A newly hired Black deputy, a 16-year veteran from MPD, had accepted to instruct a class. The lieutenant and others were undoubtedly dismayed about the Chief's decision; however, they could do nothing about it.

In 1991, I was overwhelmed with joy when the Adam Shift, patrol field commander, a Black lieutenant, alerted me that I would likely transfer to a new Division. I was assigned to the Traffic Division as an investigator at the time. The lieutenant advised me that the Sheriff was forming a Training Division with a new outlook and updated approach to law enforcement training.

He emphasized the importance of me not sharing the information because rumors were floating that I was a *"Black Radical."* Wow, I was stunned. I asked, *"Who would spread a lie like that?"* He responded, *"Don't sweat it. You keep your mouth shut and wait to see what they do."* They, meaning the Sheriff and his command staff. I found the lieutenant to be a *"fair* and *trustworthy"* supervisor.

A few weeks later, I met another sharp lieutenant who advised me of the effective date I would transfer from the Traffic Division to the Training Division. I had seen him around and recognized him as a SWAT team supervisor. The lieutenant advised that he would become the Executive Officer of the newly formed Training Division headed by a retired Memphis FBI Special Agent who specialized in instructing Law & Legal subjects.

He elaborated that I would be one of five members and a secretary comprising the Training Division. The lieutenant, too, mentioned the false rumors he heard about my being a *"Black Radical."* He said, *"Welcome aboard. Forget that nonsense; we expect you to focus on the job at hand."* I was most appreciative of the confidence he showed in me.

Today, I am so grateful to have been on the ground floor of a CALEA-accredited Academy recognized as one of the best in the region. The training assignment proved rewarding and memorable to me. I proudly earned the ranks of Sergeant and Lieutenant while assigned to the Training Academy.

In September 1996, thanks to the Sheriff and executive staff, I attended the *FBI National Academy, Session 187*, at Quantico, Virginia. The FBI Academy hosted a 3-month leadership training program for national and international police officers. I always aspired to attend the FBI National Academy as a career goal. The learning and networking experiences enhanced my Law Enforcement career tremendously.

Upon returning home, I took special pride in imparting knowledge and skills gained at the FBI Academy. As a training instructor, I developed intellectually and professionally. *"Learning by teaching others"* improved my confidence enormously.

I researched resources, developed lesson plans, facilitated teaching concepts, and coordinated training aids learned in an FBI Instructor Development Class hosted by the Germantown Police Department in Germantown, Tennessee. FBI Special Agent Harold Hays *(RIP)* coordinated and instructed the course, assisted by two Special Agents from the Washington, DC headquarters. Special Agent Hays, assigned to the Memphis FBI Field Office was an accomplished professional widely known as a premier practitioner in law enforcement training.

My transition to the Sheriff's Office from the Memphis Police Department changed my attitude, refocused my policing mentality, and expanded my field of knowledge. I developed an affinity for police training and a new outlook on supervision.

Upon reviewing complaints, I discovered that white police officers allegedly biased in public interactions with Black citizens often failed to demonstrate behavioral improvement as needed. The public could easily perceive or interpret their attitudes and behaviors as racist.

For example, suppose an officer's discriminatory behavior failed to improve following Implicit Bias training. In such a case, it may indicate an officer's desire not to comply with the training activity to improve his behavior. Today, many veteran officers, black and white, face this controversial dilemma.

Absent early warning signs or frequency of occurrences, likely, little research on biases regarding field performance could show whether white officers experienced more difficulty than black officers or vice versa.

I was especially critical of *"Macho"* or *"Hot Dog"* instructors who deviated from their lesson plans to ad-lib and joke for attention, bragging with personal opinions and mocking laws, policies, or facts. Safeguarding agencies and avoiding personal liability are crucial to establishing a credible training culture for police instructors and officers.

We constantly reminded veteran and rookie officers to stay alert and take no person or situation for granted. We reinforced video actualities and survival scenarios targeting *"careless officers"* demonstrating *"complacent"* attitudes and behaviors. The survival videos proved to be *"attention grabbers"* for correcting bad habits and verifying a broken policing culture.

In reviewing disciplinary complaints, I discovered that police officers allegedly overzealous or implicitly biased in public interactions with Black citizens often failed to demonstrate behavioral improvement as needed. The public could easily perceive or interpret their attitudes and behaviors as racist.

Source:
URBAN CRIME LAB / University of Illinois at Chicago / April 23, 2021 *"Implicit Bias Training for Police"*
By Benjamin Feigenberg, Jack Glaser & Eleni Packis

> *"While officer-involved shootings are far too common from a civil rights and public policy perspective, from a statistical perspective even in large departments there are often not enough shootings each year to facilitate the sort of statistical analysis that would*

allow us to test for links with implicit bias-influenced behaviors like shooter bias. More commonplace behaviors like vehicle and pedestrian stops and searches and use of nonlethal force can be analyzed for racial disparities with considerably greater statistical power" (Feigenberg, Glaser, Packis, 2021).

I developed a likeness for the Sheriff's Office's new approach to delivering quality training consistent with policy, case law, and the latest methods and concepts. Quality training and computer technology were rapidly advancing as operational priorities to cover liabilities. The Sheriff of Shelby County clearly understood the need for training improvements to meet demands for best practices.

During the late 1980s and early 1990s, the increase in legal challenges, training liabilities, and operational deficiencies were costly. Police-involved pursuits, crashes, brutality complaints, and discriminatory practices captured local and national news headlines. The Shelby County Jail faced a federal court decree for multiple allegations and findings. Public perception, trust, and integrity were at stake; therefore, constructive changes were inevitable.

The Sheriff of Shelby County refocused departmental efforts on ceasing outdated practices, improving personnel training, and addressing *"Good Ole Boy"* attitudes and behaviors. However, many misguided deputy sheriffs resisted the attitudinal change to no avail.

In the classroom, I frequently experienced resistance from rank-and-file hardliners who took exception to the *Cultural Diversity* and *Implicit Bias* training modules. The misguided veteran deputies voiced bigoted opinions pretending that conforming to diversity and bias training impeded their efforts to perform as the *"real police."*

They challenged the allotted in-service – diversity and bias -- training hours (2 to 4) as a waste of time. I explained that the Sheriff's Academy delivered the curricula as required by the *P.O.S.T. Commission (Peace Officers Standards & Training)* in Nashville, Tennessee. I then suggested that police officers needed more *Cultural Diversity, Implicit Bias,* and *De-escalation* training to safely manage public encounters, domestic violence, and situational outcomes. Many public complaints and civil lawsuits against Tennessee deputy sheriffs and police officers supported my suggestion.

I viewed the hardliner's biased assessments and excuses as absurd, and lacking common sense. Their warped opinions presumably represented similar opinions and subcultures shared by other misguided officers nationwide.

During in-service class sessions, several deputies chose to test my *"professional patience"* by attempting to read newspapers, which was a classroom rule violation. Because of their seniority, I imagined the veteran deputies felt I was intimidated not to correct their indifferent and insulting behavior. They were surprisingly mistaken. I perceived their disruption and rudeness as a foolhardy caper to rattle and belittle me before the other deputies.

I immediately paused my lecture and firmly ordered the newspapers put away. I purposely avoided formal disciplinary action on three occasions. Instead, I addressed the responsible deputies with choice words, gaining attention to the Academy rules and sending a strong message to others. The news eventually circulated with a clear understanding that I was no pushover. No further corrections were necessary.

6 Hearts & Minds

As a Black police officer, I asked, *"What motivates misguided police officers to perpetrate racial bias?"* I answered, *"Their motivation underscores inherent bias, ignorance, or white privilege mainly against Black people historically viewed and disrespected as inferior and subhuman by white supremacists."*

The cultural shame of racial hypocrisy and extremism in Law Enforcement rests with sympathetic sheriffs, police chiefs, subordinates, and politicians clinging to tradition, power, and control. Identifying and understanding the need for a change of *"Hearts & Minds"* are crucial to eradicating the *"Us vs. Them"* and *"Warrior"* mindsets that perpetuate racist attitudes and abusive behaviors.

As we strive to correct a broken policing culture, we cannot overlook that many police officers are unaware of their implicit biases. According to the *National Institute of*

Health (NIH), *"Implicit Bias"* is a form of bias that occurs automatically and unintentionally, impacting decisions and behaviors in favor of or against one person or group compared to another.

In assessing many racial bias and brutality complaints lodged against police departments, the videos viewed were indisputable. Officers allegedly violated the rights of unarmed Black victims. In many cases, unchecked biases led to standard practices that provoked costly civil lawsuits, impeding progress in race relations. Profoundly, I observed *"more"* than *"less"* of my white coworkers treating people with respect regardless of skin color. However, I cannot speak the same for the behavior of several white commanders I experienced.

The usual *"Unconscious Bias"* claimed by police officers is generally a weak excuse or cover by officers who refuse to correct their bias or abusive behavior. Police officers are agents of public trust accountable to the highest standards of ethical conduct.

Following my transition from the Memphis Police Department to the Shelby County Sheriff's Office, it puzzled me why some white coworkers resented my presence. I was only a 16-year patrolman seeking a fresh start and an equal opportunity to continue a career at another hometown agency. I am thankful *Sheriff Gene Barksdale (RIP)* afforded me the opportunity.

I withstood the racist subtleties without any significant problems. Initially, I rushed to judgment mischaracterizing several coworkers who later earned my respect. Nonetheless, I realized I was my worst enemy; you cannot judge a book by its cover. You must read and understand it before forming warped opinions.

However, my Law Enforcement career progressed with a strong work ethic and common sense. My attentiveness to detail resulted in three rank promotions: *Sergeant, Lieutenant,* and *Captain.* Moreover, in 1996, I cherished a rewarding opportunity to attend and graduate from the *FBI National Academy, Session 187,* at Quantico, Virginia.

The phrase *"Misguided Hearts & Minds"* represented abusive white officers who frequently patrolled or investigated crimes in high-crime Black communities. As a result, many white officers wrongly viewed or labeled *"All"* Black people as criminals.

I often witnessed this discriminatory behavior perpetrated by white patrol officers or detectives during public encounters with Black people in underserved communities. I saw and heard misguided white officers disrespectfully refer to Black elderly citizens as *"Boy"* or *"Girl"* in the presence of their children or other relatives.

I soon discovered that misguided *"Hearts & Minds"* of police officers, naive or abusive, prevailed as problematic nationwide. There were Black officers, too, who demonstrated lousy attitudes and abusive behavior doing their jobs. Many Black officers chose to adopt the *"Us vs. Them"* or *"Warrior"* mindset to ensure acceptance by White officers.

As a patrolman, I witnessed multiple racially biased public interactions with narrow-minded officers who showed no remorse or shame. I chose not to complain to my supervisors because of being distrusted or labeled a *"whiner"* or *"snitch."* Then, I felt this was the wisest thing to do because the odds of protecting my job were not in my favor as a Black officer. As a supervisor, I often corrected such offensive interactions discreetly with discussion and counseling.

I recall working with white patrol partners who repeatedly demonstrated abusive behavior to harm others physically. Subsequently, I never observed any calculated racist hatred with black partners desiring to harm others physically. Most black partners and I discreetly discussed the white coworkers who we identified as racially biased.

I recall two Memphis Police partners admitting and apologizing for their attitudes and behavior toward blacks, urging me to *"pull their coattails"* the next time. Trust and common sense helped us to understand each other and accept responsibility for any wayward *"out of bounds"* behavior.

Occasionally, one partner joked about it. He said, *"Yarbrough, how am I doing now? Keep me straight, partner."* I responded, *"You are doing great; keep it up."* He and I, of course, shared that kind of trusted partnership. Unfortunately, that was not the case with several others.

Another disturbing incident involving a Sheriff's Office white partner annoyed me. This teachable situation became a *"self-control"* experience for me while temporarily assigned as a shift training officer. I was selected to familiarize a veteran deputy sheriff with the Patrol Division's new operations and offense reporting procedures. The veteran deputy transferred to the Patrol Division from a County Jail assignment. Things had changed somewhat since he last worked in the Patrol Division.

One morning, working the Adam Shift, District 2, we were dispatched to a Burglary call at a Black complainant's residence. As the training officer, I drove the patrol unit.

On arrival, the female complainant invited us to sit at her kitchen table to document the report details. This report-taking situation was ideal for training. It allowed my partner to interact comfortably with the complainant while completing the new Offense Report form.

I pointed out two corrections on the report form at the kitchen table to avoid further errors in the following sections. My partner became frustrated with my oversight in the complainant's presence, as indicated by his facial expression. I pretended as if not to notice his frustration.

Upon returning to the patrol unit, my partner voiced resentment at my correcting him at the kitchen table. I maintained self-control giving him no reason to cast any aspersion about my oversight to anyone, mainly our supervisors, who were his good friends.

I believe my partner felt extremely comfortable voicing his resentment toward me for three reasons:

1.) *His friendship with high-level commanders.*

2.) *I was black.*

3.) *The female complainant was black.*

Perhaps, he perceived my oversight as overbearing, or he wanted it to appear that he oversaw me. Whatever prompted his frustration towards me, I assessed it as secondary to properly completing the Burglary report. I stayed focused on carrying out my training responsibilities.

My partner's resentment did not intimidate or provoke me. As mentioned, he viewed my oversight as possibly *"embarrassing"* inside the Black complainant's home. Nevertheless, I considered his attitude and behavior absurdly prompted by *implicit bias.*

Years later, the veteran deputy became my immediate commander after my promotion to Captain. However, he never took the time to meet with me constructively about any Homeland Security details under his command. Strangely, he telephoned me shortly before I transferred to the Civil Field/Levy Division and asked, *"Have you heard any rumors about your transferring to Civil?"* I said, "No, I have not." I asked myself, "Why would my immediate commander ask me that question about a transfer?" If anybody should know about a transfer for me, he should.

Ironically, his *"misguided mindset"* and *"unwillingness"* to discuss divisional operations with me were points of contention that helped me to appreciate knowing how to treat subordinates with respect. None of our telephone communications lasted three minutes at any time.

Nevertheless, I learned how to intelligently manage the shortcomings of other Sheriff's Office commanders whose leadership skills left much to desire. Many lacked integrity and credibility, primarily existing on political, school, or family connections. They failed to realize their deficiencies in supervising subordinates who did not look like them. They appeared not to care whatsoever. Above all, *Implicit Bias* contaminated their *Hearts & Minds*.

7 *Now Is the Time*

Racist strands in policing run deep in American history. *"From the beginning, there's been negative relations between police and communities of color,"* says Lorenzo Boyd, a police consultant, trainer, and vice president of diversity and inclusion at the University of New Haven. *"From slave patrols through the Civil War, Jim Crow period, the Civil Rights movement, Racial Profiling, Stop-and-Frisk, and on through the current Black Lives Matter protests"* (Volk, 2021).

Now is the time. *"Policing in America"* must sustain trust, integrity, and accountability in the public interest of equal justice and best practices. How well do I remember the racial discrimination I faced during my early law enforcement career?

Arguably, systemic racism remains the most significant cultural dilemma faced in the United States of America.

Nonetheless, law enforcement officers must never show favor to racial discrimination or supremacy – in any form – to deprive, oppress, or abuse any race of people.

Today, the unreasonable, excessive deadly force against unarmed Black victims continues to increase, provoking clarion calls for police reforms. Public complaints alleging police brutality call for prompt attention, thorough investigation, and transparency. Police abuse of any kind is unacceptable, period.

Perhaps, the following operational perspective is a no-brainer for sheriffs and police chiefs. No supervision and accountability for specialized units allow misguided subordinates to run amuck with *"wolfpack mentalities"* and abusive practices during field operations in hot-spot crime areas. Documented accountability for supervisory and subordinate personnel must be a requirement.

To curb the disproportionate use of deadly force against unarmed Black victims by misguided police officers, I suggest the U.S. Congress pass a federal law enacting a national policy requiring police agencies to comply. Despite opposition, I believe that *federal law* and a *National Standardized Policy* would draw attention to improve our broken policing culture directly. Police agencies refusing to cooperate would automatically revoke their eligibility for federal grants. In America, all police agencies reportedly receive Federal Grant Assistance.

Now is the time for misguided police officers and politicians to stop conveniently threatening Democracy with racial hate, bigotry, and ignorance. Too many remain attracted to extremist political beliefs and conspiracy theories, defying the rights of others and eroding public trust. According to FBI reports, right-wing political extremists and radicals continue infiltrating police agencies with rebellious agendas.

Meanwhile, as a boy, my *Granddaddy* frequently left me spellbound listening to the captivating stories of racial maltreatment his dad, mother, and siblings suffered while sharecropping on oppressive plantations around Red Banks and Byhalia, Mississippi. Like others, this Black family labored to do what they had to do for survival, praying fervently for favorable opportunities and living conditions.

I am incredibly blessed to boast of the Black family guidance that directed my youth development. The parental wisdom boosted my insight into the importance of doing the right thing for the right reasons and overcoming racial barriers in Memphis, my hometown. I overcame insurmountable odds to survive segregated times and abusive police officers to become a Memphis police officer, enforcing the law and maintaining public order.

As a young patrol officer, I developed an affinity for community-oriented policing, mentoring marginalized young people to become law-abiding citizens instead of incarcerated criminals. Amid criticism, I worked to change negative attitudes, build mutual trust, and establish relationships between Black citizens and police officers. My compassionate approach became a reliable trademark gaining young people's and adults' trust and cooperation.

However, thanks to *Granddaddy*, I never made excuses or allowances for lawbreakers who committed crimes or disrespected law and order. Other Black police officers probably could share similar experiences that prepared them to help others overcome criminal temptations and beat the odds.

My parents always reminded me to trust GOD; do right; and respect and treat others like I desired to be respected and treated. I am grateful for *Granddaddy's* and *Lil Mama's* parental guidance and moral wisdom that kept me focused on pursuing a crime-free and quality life. I stayed grounded in religious faith, common sense, and respect for law and order.

Meanwhile, I remember when grocery store cashiers asked customers whether they desired *"paper bags"* or *"plastic bags"* to bag their purchased items. It sounds corny, but this simple domestic improvement was a step in the right direction to accommodate effective upgrades for retail merchants, mainly grocery stores. Comparably, I wish racial progress had evolved as smoothly as grocery bags.

Nevertheless, now is the time; common sense reforms are critical for beneficial change in race relations.

Likewise, white supremacists must accommodate social and political changes for the better in American Democracy. They must see the *"big picture"* to understand how racial hate, bigotry, and ignorance erode Democracy in a civil society. Racial decency and harmony must displace hypocrisy and hatred, like *"plastic bags"* replaced *"paper bags."* The reduced expense for merchants benefited customers with more protective and less cumbersome bags for carry-out items.

Nevertheless, race relations have evolved gradually from one extreme to another, good and not-so-good. Much improvement awaits in race relations and best practices by police departments. One might ask a reasonable question, *"How can we improve race relations in cities where violent crimes and gun deaths are soaring?"*

The increased frequency of gun violence in urban cities primarily results from Black-on-Black crimes, prompting citizens to flee to suburban communities. Perhaps, the more fortunate citizens who scurry to suburban towns will likely disparage the less fortunate ones trapped in crime-infested urban cities.

White privilege-thinking citizens will likely boast of their *Second Amendment* right to bear arms, showing indifference toward citizens who reside among criminals who conveniently access guns and commit crimes. Law-abiding citizens must speak out and hold legislators accountable for sensible gun safety laws to control gun access.

Seemingly, influential, sanctimonious citizens will not speak out because they are unlikely to be gun crime victims. Many maintain a false sense of security about crime. Wake up, America; crime is rampant nationwide with no respect for a person or place.

I often debated such conversations with white and black partners about the growing problem of gun violence in urban cities and towns. Nonetheless, I conceded reluctantly. Admittedly, violent crime reflects shamefully on the quality of life in urban Black communities.

Meanwhile, many social and political changes have improved Black lives since the sharecropping hard times *Granddaddy* and his family experienced in Mississippi. I wish he and *Lil Mama* were alive to witness the comparable progress made in race relations.

In 2023, how glad both would be to see a Black sheriff and female police chief serving simultaneously in Memphis and Shelby County. The same places where *Granddaddy* once characterized *"most"* white police officers as *"rotten to the core."* He always instructed me to *"do right and stay out of their way."*

However, another critical question surfaces, *"Whatever happened to the freedom, liberty, and equality promised by America, the sweet land of liberty?"* Racial injustice remains afoot under many circumstances, explicitly and implicitly, denying marginalized citizens equal justice and opportunity.

Notably, America *"defaulted"* on the promises the Founding Fathers proclaimed in the Declaration of Independence and the United States Constitution. Equal justice for Black Americans remains a *"promissory note,"* promised, ignored, and lost.

I remember the famous "*I Have a Dream*" speech in Washington, DC, on August 28, 1963. Dr. Martin Luther King, Jr. informed America of its *"Promissory Note"* described by the following excerpts.

"This note was a promise that all men, yes, Black men, as well as white men, would be guaranteed the unalienable rights of life, liberty, and the pursuit of

happiness. It is obvious today that America has defaulted on this promissory note insofar as its citizens of color are concerned. Instead of honoring this sacred obligation, America has given the Negro people a bad check, a check which has come back marked insufficient funds." -- MLK

"Now is the time to make real the promises of Democracy. Now is the time to rise from the dark and desolate valley of segregation to the sunlit path of racial justice. Now is the time to lift our nation from the quick sands of racial injustice to the solid rock of brotherhood. Now is the time to make justice a reality for all of God's children." -- MLK

History indicates that the Founding Fathers, wealthy slaveholders, documented a fundamental human rights framework, promising a free society where "all men are created equal." The framework, *The Declaration of Independence,* defied the British government's rule of the original 13 American colonies and disavowed the God-given rights of enslaved Black people. The 13 colonies eventually became the United States of America, a democratic government formed by and for *We, the People.*

Today, the racial injustice plaguing America provides a reasonable premise that the Founding Fathers' human rights framework remains hypocritical, declaring *"all men"* as *"created equal."* They said one thing but did another, promoting moral failures, e.g., *"racial hatred"* and *"extremism."* Law Enforcement officers and politicians are responsible for upholding *Democracy & Justice* with public trust and moral integrity.

Reportedly, right-wing police officers are reacting to nationwide rumors that extremist militia groups are preparing for a *"Civil Race War"* between blacks and whites. How demoralizing are those conspiracy rumors, minimizing the global appeal of the *"Great Nation"* that boasts of patriotism and exceptionalism? However, nothing is taken for granted, particularly the cybercrime threats involving *artificial intelligence.*

Forward-thinking American citizens continually strive to bridge the racial divide with genuine fulfillment compared to the following *"hypocritical"* words originated and adopted by the Founding Fathers.

"We hold these truths to be self-evident, that all men are created equal, that they are endowed by their Creator with certain unalienable Rights, that among these are Life, Liberty and the Pursuit of Happiness."

I profoundly agree with the *"Optimism"* spoken by THE HONORABLE BARACK H. OBAMA, the 44th President of the United States of America; *"Underneath it all, we Americans have more in common for what unites us than divides us."*

8 *Implicit Bias*

"A man dies when he refuses to stand up for what is correct. A man dies when he refuses to stand up for justice. A man dies when he refuses to take a stand for what is true."

-- Dr. Martin Luther King, Jr.

White supremacy, a racist ideology, is an affront to American Democracy. This toxic belief system has intensified nationwide as a *"Crazy Normal"* in right-wing political circles. "Crazy Normal" is a portrayal of white supremacy I heard described by U.S. Senator Raphael Warnock (D-Georgia). Senator Warnock, a noted Baptist pastor, commands a dynamic political advocacy for civil rights and commonsense gun safety laws.

Warnock strongly opposed his GOP congressional colleagues who were apathetic in supporting Senate and House legislation to deter gun violence in America. Despite the rampant, senseless killing of innocent men, women, and children with high-capacity assault rifles, right-wing lawmakers refused to pass restrictive gun laws. Reportedly, beholden to the National Rifle Association (NRA), gun lobbyists, permitless gun laws, and extremist ideology, GOP right-wingers are an indirect menace to public safety.

I am appalled by the growing persistence of white supremacists spewing racial hate and incendiary rhetoric to incite political violence. They convincingly operate with sincere ignorance. I view it a moral travesty when racial hatred brazenly obstructs Democracy in public services at government venues. I am particularly disturbed by police or deputy sheriff commanders who allow extremist racial or political views to influence their job interactions, decisions, and outcomes.

I constantly remind myself and others that America is my country, too. I was born *"Black"* and raised *"smack-dab"* in the heart of South Memphis, on the west edge of Tennessee. As a boy, I eye witnessed ruthless white police officers inflict brutality and harm on Black citizens. I survived those segregated times with parental wisdom, religious faith, and respect for law and order. Unfortunately, many others claimed the same, only to make bad choices and disgrace their name.

I pledge allegiance to *"Old Glory,"* the *"Flag"* of the United States of America, as a true patriotic citizen of Democracy who happens to be *"Black and proud"* of his ancestry. America is a sovereign Democracy, *"One Nation Under God, Indivisible ..."* built on the backs of enslaved Black people. The enslavers mocked Black people as inferior, robbing them of freedom and liberty with the cruelty of *lynching, torturing, raping,* and *forced breeding.* Black Americans have suffered and sacrificed to legitimately earn a rightful stake in our American Democracy with valor and virtue.

Source:
CENTER for LAW and SOCIAL POLICY/*CLASP/*
February 26, 2020
"African American Workers Built America"
By Asha Banerjee and Cameron Johnson

> *"Black labor has been foundational to the growth of America and our economy. Enslaved people built the country's early infrastructure and produced lucrative commodities such as cotton and tobacco" (Banerjee & Johnson, 2020).*

Like others, I resented the pain and suffering withstood by Black people under the oppression of enslavers. However, I harbor no hostility or vengeance other than speaking the truth and respecting others, regardless of race, ethnicity, skin color, or political views. I rose above the racial hypocrisy, extremism, and hate that stain the fabric of our Democracy and the essence of Law Enforcement. I challenge others to do the same.

Today, why should I be expected to succumb to white supremacy and white privilege with mental subservience and moral silence? I stand boldly, too, for other Black law enforcement retirees who share my likeness and views with similar experiences. We, too, are patriotic citizens sharing a free, multiracial nation governed by Democracy and the Rule of Law.

I heard SMOKEY ROBINSON, a legendary Black singer, songwriter, and record producer, proudly say during a Chris Wallace CNN interview, *"America is my home. I am a Black American, born and raised in Detroit, Michigan."* His spoken affirmation is an undeniable fact. In other words, Smokey fortified his legitimate stake in America, not another country.

Godly blessed, Smokey exalted his musical and songwriting talents to greater heights, sharing American patriotism and exceptionalism and captivating fans worldwide. I was impressed by the honesty and confidence of a talented Black man who rose from humble beginnings and overcame racial drawbacks in a famous city and hypocritical Democracy.

However, Smokey wanted it clearly understood that he treasured *"honor and respect"* for his Black ancestors who were born and captured in Africa. Slave traders brought them to America, where white oppressors marketed them like livestock under tyrannical enslavement.

This white supremacy mentality and racist dehumanization of Black people would normalize and transform to sustain systemic racism and subvert Democracy to the present day. The historical enslavement of Black people motivated me to maximize an opportunity to create awareness, encourage learning, and promote healing. My aim seeks to expose the truth and move beyond racial hypocrisy and hate.

Meanwhile, in America today, the moral integrity of unethical police commanders, extremist subordinates, and radicalized politicians has decayed considerably, undermining the people-power in our representative Democracy. Many are unaware of their inherent racial bias. They have engaged in the same behavior for so long that they think they are doing the right thing for the right reason. I suggest that social media platforms, right-wing radio talk shows, and hate-spewing politicians have elevated *implicit bias* and *racial bigotry* in our diverse society.

Screening and hiring ethical police officers are crucial to improving policing culture, promoting best practices, and assuring equal justice with dignity and respect for all races and ethnicities. However, preventing crime, building trust, and sustaining an accountable policing culture are priorities in a multicultural Democracy.

During my career, I learned that police commanders and subordinates who view people of color as inferior allow their inherent biases and political views to influence workplace decisions. Particularly those consumed by political rhetoric, racial demagoguery, and conspiracy theories. My experiences may echo similar racially biased incidents experienced by other Black police commanders nationwide.

In December 2018, BAILEY MARYFIELD, M.S., wrote a Justice Research & Statistics Association (JRSA) news article entitled *"Implicit Racial Bias,"* introducing the following.

> *"It is important to distinguish implicit racial bias from racism or discrimination. Implicit biases are associations made by individuals in the unconscious state of mind. This means that the individual is likely not aware of the biased association" (Maryfield, 2018).*

> *"Implicit racial bias can cause individuals to unknowingly act in discriminatory ways. This does not mean that the individual is overtly racist, but*

rather that their perceptions have been shaped by experiences and these perceptions potentially result in biased thoughts or actions" (Maryfield, 2018).

"No one is immune from having unconscious thoughts and associations, but becoming aware of implicit racial bias creates an avenue for addressing the issue" (Maryfield, 2018).

<u>Example 1:</u>
Implicit Bias, or Not?

I treasured an affinity for my Sheriff's Academy assignment as a Tennessee P.O.S.T. Certified Law Enforcement Instructor. Motivating deputy sheriff recruits, instructing basic concepts, and convincing veteran officers of *Survival Awareness* appeared to be my forte.

I started as the only Black instructor on the Law Enforcement training team partnering with the Correctional or Jail training team. Over ten years, I *"ate and slept"* training with a commitment to excellence in improving the Shelby County Sheriff's Office. As an instructor and team player, I was devoted to making a difference with an unselfish spirit. Eventually, I lost confidence in the Director of Training, a retired Federal Special Agent. He appeared leery of my openness and exuberance during staff meetings and one-on-one discussions.

While attending the FBI National Academy at Quantico, Virginia, I conceived an excellent idea to benefit the Sheriff's Academy back home. The FBI Academy's *"Hogan's Alley"* practical training model fascinated me immensely.

"Hogan's Alley" was a mini-city installation for realistic, practical law enforcement training. The mini-city installation modeled residential structures, commercial businesses, designated lots, sidewalks, fire hydrants, marked streets, traffic lights, stop signs, etc. The realistic training model emphasized respective agency policy compliance while identifying the participants' performance strengths and weaknesses.

Upon returning home, I submitted a proposal for review and consideration to the Director of Training. I titled the proposal, *"Survival City,"* mirroring the *"Hogan's Alley"* practical training model.

The proposal included a drawn layout to reinforce the proposed idea. I was anxious to meet with the Director for his opinion, knowing that enough land space surrounded the Sheriff's Academy to construct a realistic training installation. I recommended soliciting corporate and private donors to sponsor the business facades, with logo signage, supporting Sheriff's Office training as community crime-prevention partners.

As time passed, the Director never responded to me about the proposal. One evening shortly after regular working hours, I entered the Academy's copy room to discover the Secretary copying the *"Survival City"* proposal.

I immediately noticed the Director had altered the proposal with several words and phrases, replacing my name with the Director as the originator. The Secretary had exited the copy room, waiting for the copier to stop. When the copier stopped, I quickly copied the altered proposal without her knowing. The coincidence stunned me.

I later showed the altered and original copies for verification to the Academy's executive captain and the Pistol Range's lieutenant. I suspected the Director intended to avoid discussing the proposal with me. I sensed he was preparing to take credit for my idea. I never said anything to him or heard anything else about the proposal. The *"Survival City"* realistic, scenario training installation never materialized.

I maintained a copy of the original proposal and the altered copy with the changes. It puzzled me why the Academy director arbitrarily changed the proposal without meeting me. As my frustrations arose, I decided to visit and discuss my concerns with the Assistant Chief, who maintained oversight of the Sheriff's Academy.

After hearing the details of my frustration, the Assistant Chief said, *"Yarbrough, do you know what you need to do?"* I said, *"No, sir."* He said, *"You just need to pray. I think that might help your frustration."* I respectfully thanked him for his time and advice.

Nevertheless, I felt deflated and discouraged upon leaving the Assistant Chief's downtown office. His response opened my eyes in a way I will never forget. As a Black deputy sheriff, regardless of status, I learned a teachable life lesson that strengthened me in facing sensitive workplace challenges. Again, I reflected on *Granddaddy's* and *Lil Mama's* wisdom, *"Birds of the same feather flock together."* The same holds for circumstances of implicit bias, in most cases, even though disagreement may be apparent.

In 2000, the Patrol Division's Inspector and Captain visited me three times at the Academy, asking if I would be interested in becoming the Field Commander (lieutenant) for the Baker Patrol Shift. They felt my leadership capability would perfectly steer the evening shift in the right direction. I was highly flattered by the confidence shown in me.

Nonetheless, I repeatedly turned down the opportunity because I did not want it to seem as if I undermined the Shift Commander already in place. After that, my Academy frustrations with the Director increased, prompting me to reconsider the transfer opportunity.

<u>Example 2:</u>

Implicit Bias, or Not?

In 2011, after assuming command of the Sheriff's Civil Field/Levy Division from Homeland Security, I often suspected the Assistant Chief of discriminatory behavior, particularly during in-office meetings. I perceived his dogmatic assertions as detrimental to employee morale and the Sheriff's Office's core values.

I am pleased to share another unforgettable experience surrounding a disciplinary suspension that involved me. The firsthand experience evaluated my Godly faith and job dedication. It was a first-time experience for me. The suspension marred my integrity, insulted my intelligence, and defamed my reputation as a supervising employee.

Assistant Chiefs are executive commanders directly influencing their respective departments' ethical values and best practices. Their decisions determine the actions of subordinates and how outcomes resolve. In other words, what will happen? I contend that most subordinates perceive what Assistant Chiefs say as not as important as what they do. I believe ethical leaders must constantly perform as role models for all subordinates.

When summoned to my Assistant Chief's office many times, I observed that he regularly listened to the *"Rush Limbaugh Show,"* a popular, right-wing, nationally syndicated political talk radio show. I perceived his listening as likely to unjustly influence his workplace interactions and decisions. Reportedly, Limbaugh was known for spewing extremist ideology and political rhetoric favored by white supremacists.

Upon entering the office, I could see and hear the radio from atop a credenza behind his office desk. Each time, he lowered the volume or turned off the radio. On duty, I viewed his listening to the Limbaugh political talk show as hypocrisy. Because he frequently reminded subordinates to avoid the mere appearance of political indulgence on duty.

Similar incidents mirroring the following circumstances of my wrongful suspension go unchecked by sympathetic police chiefs and sheriffs. They typically look the other way, ignoring wrongdoing likely to encourage subordinates to make lousy choices or consider acts of misconduct. Their blind eye is counterproductive to improving a broken policing culture.

I strongly advocate for police officers to remain politically neutral and avoid radical thinking and abusive behaviors that violate the rights of others. Noticeably, my Assistant Chief seemed obsessed with portraying an authoritarian *"know-it-all"* attitude when meeting with Black subordinates.

The Assistant Chief was oblivious to the operational difficulty in abruptly switching a field sergeant's duties to an administrative sergeant's tasks. The switch required the field sergeant to train for the administrative sergeant's tasks and responsibilities. As a result of disinformation, my Assistant Chief wanted to satisfy several disgruntled part-time employees (friends) he hired. I discovered they misled him with blatant lies and false assumptions.

Reportedly, several part-timers disliked the Black field sergeant due to his insistence that the part-time officers increase their work productivity. The Civil Division's paper counts (process not served) had increased in the districts assigned to the part-timers. However, the Black field sergeant intelligently disregarded their nonsense and maintained his insistence.

Commending the cooperative spirit of my supervisors proved to be a winning strategy for increasing work productivity. We smartly refocused to adjust districts and schedules for the timely service of court-ordered process and proper return of levy executions. We worked hard to maintain positive working relationships between in-office and field personnel.

As Captain, on-site, overseeing an estimated workforce of 50 employees, I consciously identified operational strengths, weaknesses, and needs. To boost morale, I promoted the cliché that *"Employees don't work for me; they work with me."*

I reported to two commanders, a White assistant chief, and a Black chief inspector, who once worked for me as a lieutenant. I consistently kept them apprised of all relevant operational details. Their offices were off-site at the downtown headquarters.

I will never forget when both commanders rushed to judgment and charged me with *"INSUBORDINATION"* for inadvertently disobeying an order prompted by concocted lies and false assumptions pushed by part-time employees. My two commanders' shallow thinking and disrespect for my Captain's rank and Civil Division's command position were despicably unprofessional and willfully vengeful.

Nevertheless, the disgruntled part-timers disregarded my authority and the chain of command. I received information that they met regularly with my Assistant Chief for early morning breakfast, undermining the Black field sergeant.

Disinformation was provided directly to the Assistant Chief by the part-time employees (deputy sheriff process servers) upset with the Black field sergeant. Strangely, the part-timers never made any verbal or written complaints to any of the Civil Division sergeants or the female lieutenant about workplace problems or disciplinary violations.

The Black field sergeant informed me that the disgruntled white part-timers were friends of our Assistant Chief, who hired them upon retirement from the Memphis

Police Department (MPD). He once worked with the part-timers at MPD. They became angry, alleging that the Black field sergeant *"did not know how to talk to the officers"* during roll call briefings. Supposedly, the Sergeant *"disrespected"* the part-timers.

During a meeting in his office, the Assistant Chief asked me, *"What's going on out there? Some folks are telling me what's going on. They told me about a Sergeant who doesn't know how to talk to the officers at roll call."* I replied, *"Wow, I am unaware of any complaints or rumors. Nobody has reported anything to me."*

He responded loudly, *"I want that Field Sergeant moved to the Administrative Sergeant's position out there."* Again, I stared in awe because I knew training a field sergeant to cover an administrative sergeant's tasks would take longer. Their in-office duties and responsibilities contrasted significantly. The Assistant Chief's insistence indicated that he was out of touch with the operational capabilities of the Administrative Sergeant's position.

He suddenly deflected to another issue when I explained that I needed more time. I never said I would not comply with the Assistant Chief's request. Moments later, I respectfully advised him that I would investigate and report my findings. However, he seemed disinterested.

A day later, I emailed a memo to both commanders suggesting a recommendation and confirming that the supervisors had reported no complaints. Strangely, I received no response from either commander.

About two weeks later, the Black chief inspector served me with official suspension papers. He formally relieved me of my badge, identification card, duty pistol, cellphone, hand-held radio, office keys, and take-home vehicle.

The suspension notification occurred during a monthly Key Indicators' meeting at the Sheriff's Academy to review department head activity reports. Another Chief Inspector observed the notification in the Academy director's office. I resented the timing, location, and clumsy handling of the notification. I suspected the choosing of the time and place was no coincidence. It appeared flaunted before my peers to embarrass and teach me a lesson.

I assumed the Sheriff and Chief Deputy were privy to the Assistant Chief's plan to suspend me. All attended the Key Indicator's meeting as usual. Before my disciplinary hearing, nobody interviewed me to discuss any aspects of my evidential details.

I was relieved of duty with pay extending over 20 days as the Disciplinary Review Officer (DRO) scheduled a formal hearing. The Assistant Chief assigned to conduct the formal disciplinary hearing once commanded the *Bureau of Professional Standards & Integrity (BOPSI)*.

Later, after carefully assessing the insubordination charges and evidence, the Assistant Chief *(Hearing Officer)* requested that I meet him at the Sheriff's Academy. The Black chief inspector would attend the meeting, too.

During the meeting, the Hearing Officer advised me that he dismissed the disciplinary suspension and charges filed against me. He explained the charges did not justify the corrective action taken. I submitted a 29-page report of documentation, memos, emails, text messages, etc., defending my decisions and contradicting the charges. I respectfully requested that the BOPSI case information be removed from my main personnel file. I had endured a lengthy and stressful ordeal that was wrong, demeaning, and unnecessary.

Without discussion or notice, my assistant chief allowed the Black chief inspector to fulfill his vengeful agenda charging me with *"Insubordination."* This abuse of authority appeared personal. Both were hell-bent on *"teaching me a lesson,"* refusing to consider anything I said about the disinformation they received from disgruntled part-time employees.

I quickly recognized that the Black chief inspector seemingly demonstrated a *"puppet mentality"* carrying out the assistant chief's disciplinary verdict against me. His subservient demeanor proved disgusting. He seemed on a mission to maintain favor with the assistant chief and the sheriff. I viewed his subservient behavior as reflective of a typical workplace cliché, *"Go Along to Get Along,"* undermining others to remain in good graces for personal gain.

Consequently, my attempt to explain the valid reason for not immediately swapping out the administrative sergeant's tasks was unacceptable to my assistant chief. He refused to hear my recommendation to avoid monthly report errors resulting from the field sergeant's lack of administrative training. The assistant chief completely discounted my justification. I needed more time to train the field sergeant to avoid inaccurate reports and records representing my ultimate responsibility as the Civil Division commander.

To summarize, I revealed workplace experiences exposing racial prejudice due to inherent bias, political views, and peer pressure. I believe the dispositions or outcomes of the experiences embraced white supremacy ideology and sincere ignorance. In essence, when *Implicit Bias* is perpetrated in government service environments by command, supervisory, or management personnel, overt discrimination thrives continuously.

9 "Wake Up, America"

"Wake up, America." We, the People, must preserve Democracy and rebuke our broken policing culture, toxic politics, and systemic racism. Throw *Racial Hypocrisy, Hatred,* and *Ignorance* out of the window. *Moral Decay* spoils the essence of a *"perfect Union,"* as introduced by the *Preamble to the United States Constitution. Moral Decay* deteriorates integrity, specifically exposing police officers and politicians who fail to distinguish right and wrong.

In closing, American Democracy was formed by and for *We, the People,* in a free society promising life, liberty, and the pursuit of happiness. In a constitutional Democracy, I suggest that *"Uncle Sam"* – love him or not -- urges *"the People"* to live, work, and play together in peace and harmony. Now is a good time. We can – and must – do better. Tomorrow promises nothing. Nevertheless, I remain anxious with optimism.

Uncle Sam, a nickname depicting the United States of America, metaphorically, stands as a cartoon symbol of patriotism and exceptionalism. According to the National Geographic Society, *"Uncle Sam has been a long-standing symbol of American patriotism. His image has been used by the United States government in different ways, from stamps and military recruiting posters to magazines and newspaper cartoons."*

The United States of America is a multiracial, multicultural, democratic nation undeserving of the *racial hypocrisy, hatred, and ignorance* that tarnish Democracy. Ultimately, we must denounce and expose *"Racial Hate"* because of *"Ignorance." Racial Hate & Ignorance* anywhere is an enemy to human rights everywhere.

Americans must establish meaningful relationships and reinforce our humanity with truth and understanding. When we hate others, we waste too much valuable time sowing hate from one to the other. Time is a terrible waste when much work requires racial reconciliation in a diverse society of free people.

We, the People, must take the time to immerse in honest discourse and a clear realization of the truth about American History before subjugating Black citizens. Racial hypocrisy blindfolds Democracy, stoking societal fears with *hatred* and *ignorance* to sustain white supremacy and political dominance. Arguably, extremists waste valuable time for the wrong reasons.

We, the People, constantly pretend that Democracy has evolved -- for the better -- overshadowing years of demoralizing Black people with enslavement, terror, and cruelty. Accordingly, racist political agendas, social media extremism, and undisputable actualities exposing a broken policing culture show differently. Today, similar attitudes and decisions that justified slavery and lynching continue to defy Democracy under the shameless passion of *"White Supremacy"* and *"White Nationalism."*

Shame, shame, shame. Misguided police officers *(Bad Apples)* repeatedly inflame a broken policing culture with implicit and explicit biases undermining Democracy with abusive attitudes and practices. Police officers are *"Guardians"* of Democracy, representing the faces of multiracial communities, cities, and towns, serving, protecting, and enforcing the rule of law.

As mentioned, the *Rule of Law* is the bedrock of American Democracy. Law-abiding, open-minded, taxpaying citizens expect police officers to manifest trust, integrity, and respect without misguided exceptions, excuses, or assumptions.

As America tolerates the persistence of white supremacy, Black Americans must *"speak up and speak out,"* never cowering to racial degradation, inferiority, or mockery. There must not be any inclination to appease the immoral practices of misguided whites by compromising dignity or credibility. In a multiracial society, cultural dominance by one race, group, or class of people defeats the democratic premise of constitutional Democracy.

We, the People, must repent of the enslavement and lynching inflicted on Black people like the Founding Fathers demanded freedom and liberty from England's rule of the thirteen colonies. According to an old English proverb, *"What is good for the goose is good for the gander."* As patriotic Americans, we demonstrate repentance by establishing racial and social relationships with mutual trust and respect for one to the other.

Strangely, the Founding Fathers had no problem enslaving Black people to maintain white supremacy, wealth, and power. They ignored their abhorrent transgressions denying freedom and liberty to enslaved Black people, considered inferior and subhuman.

Nowhere does the *Preamble to the U.S. Constitution* deny or favor a particular race, group, or class of people embraced by Democracy. It promotes "*We, the People,*" with pride, inclusion, and equality imperative for the shared bond of native-born and naturalized American citizens.

The Preamble to the United States Constitution

"We, the People of the United States, in Order to form a more perfect Union, establish Justice, ensure domestic Tranquility, provide for the common defense, promote the general Welfare, and secure the Blessings of Liberty to ourselves and our Posterity, do ordain and establish this Constitution for the United States of America."

In the United States of America, our democratic government boasts that *all men are created equal* under the rule of law. Consequently, Democracy crumbles without the rule of law. When Democracy falters, *"Us vs. Them"* mindsets and *"Warrior"* mentalities fester to sustain a broken policing culture.

Too many misguided police officers and politicians have little or no concept of right and wrong when it involves minority people, particularly Black people. They do not care. Inherent biases blind them. Both public servants have long neglected their oath of office with implicit practices of racial hypocrisy, hatred, and ignorance, believing they were right.

Consequently, white supremacy threatens Democracy by contaminating social and political discourse with extremist ideology. Unfortunately, as a nation formed on democratic principles and values, we inherited a cancerous history of cruelty, injustice, and hatred targeting Black people. We, the People, must learn and move responsibly beyond the oppressive past.

Sworn police officers and elected officials should uphold Democracy and enforce the rule of law fairly and impartially. Since the founders framed the Declaration of Independence and the U.S. Constitution, that proposition has too often subverted Democracy.

In 2017, the Equal Justice Initiative (EJI), headed by well-known Attorney Brian Stevenson in Montgomery, Alabama, published a comprehensive report entitled *"Lynching in America: Confronting the Legacy of Racial Terror (3rd Edition)."* The information introduced that *"During the period between the Civil War and World War II, thousands of African Americans were lynched in the United States. Lynchings were violent public acts of torture that traumatized Black people throughout the country, largely tolerated by state and federal officials."* The lynchings reportedly *"peaked between 1880 and 1940."*

Then and now, structural racism never benefitted Black Americans as endorsed by misguided bureaucrats and legislators. During earlier years, Law Enforcement's blind eye and indifference played a dreadful role in aiding and abetting lynching and terrorism at the *"beck and call"* of ruthless white mobs.

On November 12, 2021, Jordan Sheppard wrote an article entitled *"History focuses on men, but Black women were lynched, too,"* published by *The Howard Center for Investigative Journalism.* "Between 1865 and 1965, there were nearly 5,000 racial terror lynchings of Black people. Approximately 120 of those victims were Black women."

Little did I know that Memphis, Tennessee, my hometown, attracted national attention by lynching and terrorizing Black people based on preposterous allegations driven by *hatred* and *ignorance.* I was shocked that one lynching incident involving People's Grocery Store originated in South Memphis on *"the Corner"* of Mississippi Boulevard & Walker Avenue.

In 1892, the Black-owned grocery store occupied the southeast corner across from where Four-Way Grill, Curve Pocket Billiards, and Yarbrough's Barber Shop opened for business many years later. As I remember, circa 1953, the store's name had changed to People's Drug Store, operated by two Black pharmacists. One pharmacist's name was Dr. Pippin. Later, Dr. Pippin's partner left, and Dr. Irving arrived on the scene.

Later, People's Drug Store closed and moved immediately north next to the Four-Way Grill, reportedly at 1014 Mississippi Boulevard, under a new business name, Oriole Drug Store, operated by pharmacists Pippin and Irving.

The renowned FOUR-WAY RESTAURANT, renovated under new ownership, Jerry & Patrice Bates-Thompson, occupies the business spaces that once housed Lucius *"Heavy"* Bolden's pool room and Denver Yarbrough's barber shop. I was raised on *"the Corner"* as a young boy working in the barbershop for eight years, 1950-1958.

The iconic ACE Theater was directly across the street. Later, it closed, and the RITZ Theatre opened at the exact location. Many years ago, the famous *Mississippi Boulevard & Walker Avenue* corner was called *"the Curve."*

Source:
EQUAL JUSTICE INITIATIVE (EJI) / 2017
"Three Black Grocers Lynched in Memphis, Tennessee"

On March 9, 1892, a white mob stormed the Memphis jail, seized three Black men held inside, and brutally lynched them without trial. Earlier that year, these same three Black men—Thomas Moss, Calvin McDowell, and William "Henry" Stewart—opened the People's Grocery Company in Memphis, Tennessee. Located across the street from a white-owned grocery store that had previously had a monopoly in the local Black community, the men's new business reduced the white store's profits. The venture also threatened the racial order by forcing white businessmen to compete economically with Black businessmen (Equal Justice Initiative, 2017).

Source:
THE BENJAMIN L. HOOKS INSTITUTE for SOCIAL CHANGE at the UNIVERSITY OF MEMPHIS/September 30, 2015
"Memphis and the Lynching at the Curve"
By Nathaniel C. Ball

> *Thomas Moss symbolized the urban entrepreneurial class of African Americans that emerged in the decades following the Civil War. Moss invested in a community-owned grocery store, the People's Grocery, which he managed at night after spending his days working as a postman. The People's Grocery was located at the southeast corner of what is today Mississippi Blvd and Walker Ave, known then as "the Curve" for the distinctive turn that streetcars made at the corner. During an era in which African Americans were subject to racial subjugation, the People's Grocery stood as an emblem of pride for the community (Ball, 2015).*

The celebrated public lynchings and racial terror stoked unimaginable fear wreaking havoc to denounce justice and prosperity for Black people. The white supremacy ideology, radical attitudes, and violent behaviors that subverted the Rule of Law yesteryear remain prevalent today.

Source:
THE HISTORICAL MARKER DATABASE/Revised April 29, 2022
"The Lynching of Ell Persons"
By Bill Pfingsten

"Near this spot on May 22, 1917, a lynching party chained Ell Persons to a log, doused him in gasoline, and burned him alive. An estimated 5,000 spectators witnessed his death or viewed his remains soon afterward. Persons, a black woodcutter who lived nearby, was facing charges of raping and decapitating Antoinette Rappel, 15, a white schoolgirl last seen on her bicycle crossing the Wolf River over the Macon Road bridge. In building a case against Persons, authorities relied primarily on a coerced confession made "after a long siege of beating" and "third degree tactics" from law officers, as the Memphis press reported. Once authorities charged Persons with the slaying, they sent him to Nashville for safekeeping" (Pfingsten, 2022).

Sadly, Ell Persons, a Black man, was entangled in a web of corrupt law enforcement and doomed to the abyss of *"Memphis Justice."* Ell Persons' life amounted to zero – absolutely nothing -- in the murderous Hearts & Minds of the white mob, gloating spectators, and law enforcement officers.

> *"Meanwhile, groups of white men referred to as "the avengers" monitored all rail lines into Memphis as Person's trial date approached. On May 21, 1917, one of these groups overpowered two Shelby County deputies, seized Persons, and removed him from a rail passenger car outside Potts Camp, Mississippi. News reports in Memphis the next morning stated the time and place where Persons would be lynched. A carnival atmosphere prevailed here as automobiles jammed Macon Road and vendors sold drinks and snacks. After the lynching, onlookers dismembered Person's charred body. Later that day, his head and foot were dumped on Beale Street for black pedestrians to see. No one was brought to trial in either the Rappel or Persons slayings" (Pfingsten, 2022).*

Reportedly, 1865 to 1965 was a despicable, domineering period of lynching and racial cruelty in America, where *"Moral Decay"* prevailed among evil white people.

On May 22, 1917, Ell Persons was soaked with gasoline and burned alive for public enjoyment. This atrocious, barbaric event was depicted as *"Hell on Earth"* in Memphis, Tennessee. It spread a profound message nationwide that Southern whites rejected equal justice for Black people with vigilante lynchings and raging terror. They publicized and celebrated widespread lynchings as if attending an outdoor sports event.

As American History recalls the lynching phenomena that moved across the South, *"a $64,000 question"* comes to mind. As set forth by the Founding Fathers, where were the constitutional checks and balances to protect Democracy, equal rights, and the quality of life promised to *"ALL"* citizens? Arguably, no moral, judicial, or political leadership was apparent during this evil period of rampant lynchings and raging terror across the southern states.

Conveniently, *due process* disappeared for protecting Black defendants' legal rights and lives while in police custody. Police officers and deputy sheriffs allegedly colluded with ruthless white mobs and compromised the rule of law to condemn and murder Black people.

Comparably, today, FBI reports indicate that Law Enforcement agencies nationwide have been infiltrated by a growing number of white officers motivated by white supremacy and white nationalist ideology.

Hate killings, racially and politically motivated, and the needless shooting deaths of unarmed Black victims by misguided police officers have increased nationwide. Shame on America's pretentious subcultures of freedom, liberty, and justice. How long before *"exceptionalism"* will prove authenticated as boasted?

Meanwhile, *"Blind Democracy"* covers a broad range of racial exploitation, exposing the shame of white supremacy embedded in American Democracy. I refer to the cultural stain of *Expicit* or *"Conscious"* and *Implicit* or *"Unconscious"* biases that subjugate Black people with white privilege, control, and power.

As a boy, I harbored resentment when *Granddaddy* told me depressing stories about Mississippi sharecropping and the terror of lynching. Tears glassed my eyes. He explained how racist white people controlled Black people for political and economic gains.

Many whites remain convinced that white privilege laws should prevail, along with the return of Jim Crow segregation. Southern plantation owners manipulated impoverished Blacks to believe there was no other economic help for them besides sharecropping.

Source:
EQUAL JUSTICE INITIATIVE (EJI) / November 21, 2018
"Sharecropping"

> *"The widespread economic exploitation of the Black community continued for generations after slavery's end, due to discrimination, violence, and terrorism.*

> *In addition to convict leasing systems that re-enslaved Black people through criminalization, and lynching that enforced white supremacy through terror, sharecropping and disenfranchisement created a system of unchecked racialized economic domination"* (Equal Justice Institute, 2018).

One of *Granddaddy's* teachable stories I absorbed likely shadowed similar sharecropping misfortunes of poor Black families across the South, mainly around Red Banks and Byhalia, Mississippi. When asked where he was born, *Granddaddy* always replied, "*Somewhere between Red Banks and Byhalia.*"

I chose to mention the state of Mississippi because this is where *Granddaddy's* stories and many other true stories originated. Those early 20th-century stories reflected the domination and intimidation by white supremacists during *Granddaddy's* lifetime. White supremacy ideology continues threatening American Democracy from the 20th century to now.

Nonetheless, I contend that it is wrong for any race, group, or class of people to use their skin color, or economic status, as a privilege to violate or whitewash the human or civil rights of others. I rebuke the sharecropping incentive as manipulated to subjugate Black people because of the following story.

During my law enforcement career, I turned many negatives into positives, negating racial stereotypes meant to subjugate me. I firmly believe that whatever happens to you in life happens to you. Nevertheless, stand tall and confront adversity to beat the odds. That is the legacy *Granddaddy* left for me. I strive to pass that legacy on to others.

Granddaddy often told me how he watched his father and mother work from sunup to sundown, trying to meet family obligations to pay their sharecropping debt. He and the eight siblings did not attend regular school for several years because they plowed, planted, and harvested the plantation owner's crops. They often worked on Saturdays and Sundays, depending on the crop type.

One story I remember involved a cotton crop year when the Yarbrough family jumped for joy, celebrating a successful year. They harvested 18 bales of cotton. *Granddaddy's* mother had tallied the sharecropping debt owed to the plantation landlord. He told me his mother was more formally educated than his father. Nonetheless, much of her learning was self-taught. She excelled at reading and arithmetic, which was rare among Black families in the area.

However, the family met disappointment when they traveled to meet the landlord at the Cotton Gin. They discovered the landlord had swindled 15 bales of cotton from the family. The landlord announced that the Yarbroughs were considerably short of the 18 bales of cotton reported initially. He dared the father to submit anything else differently. The landlord forced the father to say he had made a mistake and agree to the cotton handlers' count of only *three* bales of cotton.

The deceitful landlord shouted, "*You Niggers don't have no 18 bales of cotton.*" *Granddaddy* said his father answered, "*Yes, sir, boss, that's what we had figured up.*" Another white man scolded his father, "*Nigger, are you calling that white man a lie?*" The father replied, "*No, sir, boss.*" The gross thievery of 15 bales of cotton kept the family in a financial hole with massive sharecropping debt for the coming year.

That same year the family fled the Red Banks (Marshall County) plantation one quiet night after midnight. They courageously escaped in a two-horse-drawn wagon from the plantation. The weather was clear, and the moon was bright. *Granddaddy* said the six boys were armed with Winchester rifles looking out and protecting the three sisters covered in the large wagon. The father and mother were driving the horses. They arrived safely at another sharecropping plantation in Olive Branch, Desoto County, Mississippi. The Landlord Agreement there was more accommodating for the family.

Indeed, those times were the epitome of human suffering and economic despair for most *"Negroes"* in Marshall County, Mississippi. The primary means of survival for poor *"Negroes"* in Mississippi was farming. Subsequently, the sharecropping concept was left mainly for *"Negroes."*

Gone are the days of *Granddaddy's* tearjerking stories about his experiences chopping and picking cotton in Mississippi from sunup to sundown. Nonetheless, sharecropping saved the lives of poor Black families at the expense of human inferiority and second-class citizenship.

Granddaddy watched the White folks' children attend school while he and his siblings stayed home laboring in the cotton fields. Like many poor blacks, the Yarbrough family survived harsh economic times with limited or no choices.

I once read that the sharecropping hypocrisy of wealthy, white landowners in Southern states paralleled the racial hypocrisy of the Founding Fathers and ruthless slaveholders. They amassed enormous wealth by exploiting free labor and opposing the human rights of Black people. I believe the deceitful manipulation of sharecropping -- then and now -- presents a compelling comparison.

I was struck by *Granddaddy's* passion, encouraging me always to respect and defend Black History and our family's ancestry. He suggested that I never forget the human affliction, suffering, and sacrifice weathered by Black people in America. Slavery, the Civil War, Reconstruction, and Jim

Crow eras are teachable, undeniable components of American History, sustaining the significance of and the appreciation for Democracy.

America is *"... One Nation Under GOD, Indivisible, With Liberty and Justice for All."* We must learn and share the historical sacrifices of others who came before us. The truth safeguards us from lies, false assumptions, and conspiracy theories.

Wake Up, America. The *"Sad Truth"* still haunts us as a democratic nation. White supremacy and white nationalism advocates are rising and tearing away at the moral fabric of Democracy with *racial hatred,* and *ignorance.* Arguably, they lurk with radicalized ideology, moving to sabotage Democracy for racial dominance and political power at any cost.

In the United States, the rapid rise of white supremacy and white nationalism has diminished the global perception of *American Democracy.* Both racial ideologies espouse that white people are inherently and culturally superior to Black people, representing racism and extremism in the purest forms.

Moreover, most historical perspectives suggest that the United States of America, *the sweet land of liberty,* was built on the backs of enslaved Black people. On February 12, 2015, Sven Beckert's article, *"America's first big business? Not the railroads, but slavery,"* presented on PBS News Hour, and

WKNO TV, perked interest with the following excerpt. Beckert is an American history professor at Harvard University.

> *As a group of freedmen in Virginia observed in 1867, "our wives, our children, our husbands, have been sold over and over again to purchase the lands we now locate upon. ... And then didn't we clear the land, and raise the crops of corn, of tobacco, of rice, of sugar, of everything. And then didn't the large cities in the North grow up on the cotton and the sugars and the rice that we made?" Slavery, they understood, was inscribed into the very fabric of the American economy (Beckert, 2015).*

Accordingly, *"We, the People,"* formed a sovereign, central government ruled and ratified in 1787 as a representative Democracy, distinguished by a U.S. House of Representatives and U.S. Senate Chamber. Subsequently, the total population of each state determined the formula for fair representation to Congress. In the South, each enslaved Black person counted in the population as *"three-fifths"* of a person.

Ironically, the Founding Fathers enacted democratic, constitutional legislation predicated on principles and values affirming *"All Men Are Created Equal."* However, the hypocritical founders regarded Black people as inferior, subhuman, and unworthy of any rights respected by white people.

Today, *"Blacks in America"* continue struggling for an equitable stake in Democracy compared to the Founding Founders, who declared independence from the oppressive King of England.

The founders' intolerance of British taxation ultimately led to winning the Revolutionary War in 1783 and forming the American Democracy today. However, the founders reportedly ignored over a half million enslaved Black human beings as insignificant to their quest for freedom and sovereignty.

Like yesteryear, the exact racist sentiment remains at the forefront of white supremacy and white nationalist ideology. Racial beliefs and biases degrading Black people still threaten equal justice and political discourse in American Democracy.

I characterize those beliefs and bigotry as the epitome of *ignorance and hate* undermining the future of racial justice. Sadly, for many Black and brown citizens, trusting misguided police officers, politicians, and government bureaucrats is becoming a bittersweet, foregone conclusion.

America, wake up and practice the patriotism and democratic principles and values *"We, the People,"* boast of being exceptional. Rebuke the r*acial hypocrisy* and *political ignorance* that threaten Democracy and Law Enforcement.

In the final analysis, Black Americans remain belittled by racial hypocrisy, ignorance, and hatred in all walks of life. I asked myself, *"How Free Is Free?"* This question has been unanswered for more than 150 years, since the 1865 Emancipation Proclamation, the Reconstruction period, Jim Crow segregation, and the signing of the 1964 Civil Rights Act and 1965 Voting Rights Act. Nevertheless, I remain optimistic.

REFERENCES

Alladin, T.A. (2023, March 12) *Policing has its roots in slave catching. To change it, we must change that legacy.* Retrieved from Policing has its roots in slave-catching. To change it, we must change that legacy | Opinion - Pennsylvania Capital-Star (penncapital-star.com)

Ambrose, S.E. (2002, November) *Founding Fathers and Slaveholders.* Retrieved from https://www.smithsonianmag.com/history/founding-fathers-and-slaveholders-72262393/

Anti-Defamation League, ADL (2022, May 3) *Extremism in American Law Enforcement: Far Greater Transparency, Accountability Needed.* Retrieved from https://www.adl.org/resources/report/extremism-american-law-enforcement-far-greater-transparency-accountability-needed

Ball, N.C. (2015, September 30) *Memphis and the Lynching at the Curve.* Retrieved from Memphis and the Lynching at the Curve | Uplift Memphis, Uplift the Nation: The Blog for Community Engagement

Banerjee, A., Johnson, C. (2020, February 26) *African American Workers Built America.* Retrieved from African American Workers Built America | CLASP

Beckert, S. (2015, February 12) *America's first big business? Not the railroads, but slavery.* Retrieved from America's first big business? Not the railroads, but slavery | PBS NewsHour

Cole, D., Westwood, S. (2020, May 31) *National Security Adviser: "I Don't Think There's Systemic Racism in U.S. Police Forces."*

Retrieved from https://www.cnn.com/2020/05/31/politics/robert-obrien-systemic-racism-george-floyd-cnntv/index.html

Dallas Morning News (2020, June 3) *Are Bad Apples the Problem, or is Policing Across the Country in Need of an Overhaul?* Retrieved from https://www.dallasnews.com/opinion/editorials/2020/06/03/are-bad-apples-the-problem-or-is-policing-across-the-country-in-need-of-an-overhaul/

DeSilver, D., Lipka, M., Fahmy, D. (2020, June 3) *"10 Things We Know About Race and Policing in the U.S.* Retrieved from https://www.pewresearch.org/fact-tank/2020/06/03/10-things-we-know-about-race-and-policing-in-the-u-s/

Di Liscia, V. (2020, June 18) *Historical Painting is Altered to Show Most Declaration of Independence Signatories Were Enslavers.* Retrieved from https://hyperallergic.com/572035/historical-painting-is-altered-to-show-most-declaration-of-independence-signatories-were-enslavers/

Equal Justice Initiative (EJI) (2017) *Three Black Grocers Lynched in Memphis, Tennessee.* Retrieved from On Mar 09, 1892: Three Black Grocers Lynched in Memphis, Tennessee (eji.org)

Equal Justice Initiative (EJI) (2018, November 18) *Sharecropping.* Retrieved from Sharecropping (eji.org)

Feigenberg, B., Glaser, J., Packis, E. (2021, April 23) *Implicit Bias Training for Police.* Retrieved from https://urbanlabs.uchicago.edu/attachments/a11adfec96ff6054bc4146c1d366bdf26861fcc7/store/35ceee1c8a33feebad18b35aa80f7c55c435ce0f7f9e56d6cbee40b6bf27/Implicit+Bias+Training+for+Police.pdf

Fitch, B.D. (2011, October 11) *Rethinking Ethics in Law Enforcement.* Retrieved from https://leb.fbi.gov/articles/focus/focus-on-ethics-rethinking-ethics-in-law-enforcement

Gates, H.L. (2009, February 9) *Was Lincoln a Racist?* Retrieved from https://www.theroot.com/was-lincoln-a-racist-1790868802

German, M. (2020, August 27) *Hidden in Plain Sight: Racism, White Supremacy, and Far-Right Militancy in Law Enforcement.* Retrieved from Hidden in Plain Sight: Racism, White Supremacy, and Far-Right Militancy in Law Enforcement | Brennan Center for Justice

Goldwin, R.A. (1987, May) *Why Blacks, Women, & Jews Are Not Mentioned in the Constitution.* Retrieved from https://www.commentary.org/articles/robert-goldwin/why-blacks-women-jews-are-not-mentioned-in-the-constitution/

Hassett-Walker, C. (2020, June 2) *The Racist Roots of American Policing: From Slave Patrols to Traffic Stops.* Retrieved from https://theconversation.com/the-racist-roots-of-american-policing-from-slave-patrols-to-traffic-stops-112816

Holloway, K. (2022, November 15) *White Nationalist Hate is Infiltrating Our Police.* Retrieved from https://www.thenation.com/article/society/law-enforcement-white-nationalism/

Hughes, V. (2021, July 6) *The Hypocrisy of White Supremacist and Far-Right Groups.* Retrieved from https://elm.umaryland.edu/voices-and-opinions/Voices--Opinions-Content/The-Hypocrisy-of-White-Supremacist-and-Far-Right-Groups-.php

Kanu, H. (2022, May 12) *Prevalence of white supremacists in law enforcement demands drastic change.* Retrieved from Prevalence of white supremacists in law enforcement demands drastic change | Reuters

Kaufman, A.J. (2021, April 24) *Most Police Are Good Apples.* Retrieved from https://alphanews.org/most-police-are-good-apples/

Kertscher, T. (2019, September 10) *Fact Check: Evidence Shows Most of the Men in Famous Declaration of Independence Painting Were Slaveholders.* Retrieved from https://illinoisanswers.org/2019/09/10/fact-check-evidence-shows-most-of-the-men-in-famous-declaration-of-independence-painting-were-slaveholders/

Levine, L. (2020, June 9) *Only the Good Apples in Police Departments Can Bring About Real Change.* Retrieved from ONLY THE "GOOD APPLES" IN POLICE DEPARTMENTS CAN BRING ABOUT REAL CHANGE - The Political Dish

MacFarlane, S. (2022, December 8) *Family of Fallen Capitol Police Officer Refuses to Shake Hands with McCarthy, McConnell at Medal Ceremony.* Retrieved from https://www.cbsnews.com/news/family-of-fallen-capitol-police-officer-refuses-to-shake-hands-with-mccarthy-mcconnell-at-medal-ceremony/

Malmin, M. (2012, April 1) *Changing Police Subculture.* Retrieved from https://leb.fbi.gov/articles/featured-articles/changing-police-subculture

Marx, G.T. (1995) *Police and Democracy.* Retrieved from http://web.mit.edu/gtmarx/www/poldem.html

Nittle, N.K. (2020, October 30) *The Three-Fifths Compromise in the Constitution.* Retrieved from https://www.thoughtco.com/three-fifths-compromise-4588466

Pfingsten, B. (2022, April 29) *The Lynching of Ell Persons.* Retrieved from The Lynching of Ell Persons Historical Marker (hmdb.org)

Ramesh, V. (2020, November 12) *The Dangers of Teaching American Exceptionalism.* Retrieved from https://bppj.berkeley.edu/2020/11/12/the-dangers-of-teaching-american-exceptionalism/

Reynolds, B.A. (2020, October 7) *You Can't Legislate Culture- Here's How to Really Implement Change.* Retrieved from Changing police culture is how to change behavior (police1.com)

Roberts-Miller, P. (2020, June 12) *Bad Apples, Police Brutality Reform.* Retrieved from https://www.patriciarobertsmiller.com/2020/06/12/its-a-few-bad-apples-is-an-argument-for-a-massive-re-imagining-of-police-not-an-argument-for-reform/

Seeley, J. (2020, June 8) *Training Through the Decades: What Has Changed and What Has Not.* Retrieved from https://trainingindustry.com/articles/content-development/training-through-the-decades-what-has-changed-and-what-has-not/

Sheppard, J. (2021, November 15) *History focuses on men, but Black women were lynched, too.* Retrieved from History focuses on men, but Black women were lynched, too (wordinblack.com)

Spivey, W.F. (2019, March 20) *America's Breeding Farms: What History Never Told You.* Retrieved from America's Breeding Farms: What History Books Never Told You | by William Spivey | Medium

Steyer, J.P. (2019, August 5) *Gun Control Laws Are Common Sense.* Retrieved from https://www.commonsensemedia.org/press-releases/gun-control-laws-are-common sense

Vakil, K. (2020, June 16) *The Warrior Mindset of Cops is One of the Biggest Obstacles to Police Reform.* Retrieved from https://archive.couriernewsroom.com/2020/06/16/police-culture-blocks-reform/

Volk, S. (2021, May 12) *The Enemy Within: Race and White Supremacy in American Policing.* Retrieved from https://www.rollingstone.com/culture/culture-features/racism-white-supremacy-american-policing-1167304/

Waxman, O.B. (2020, June 26) *What to the Slave is the Fourth of July? The History of Frederick Douglas Searing Independence Day Oration.* Retrieved from https://time.com/5614930/frederick-douglass-fourth-of-july/

Wetendorf, D. (2002) *Police Culture.* Retrieved from http://www.abuseofpower.info/2culture.html

Wilson, N. (2022, October 4) *Fact Sheet: Weakening Requirements to Carry a Concealed Firearm Increases Violent Crime.* Retrieved from https://www.americanprogress.org/article/fact-sheet-weakening-requirements-to-carry-a-concealed-firearm-increases-violent-crime/

ABOUT THE AUTHOR

"I cannot complain. GOD's favor sheltered and nurtured little ole me. He guided me through trying times. I am eternally grateful for His bountiful blessings: Life, Family, Grace, Goodness, and Mercy."

Denver T. Yarbrough, a native Memphian, launched his law enforcement career on March 4, 1968, with the Memphis Police Department (MPD) in Memphis, Tennessee. On January 9, 1984, Yarbrough resigned from MPD, completing 16 years of service in good standing.

On August 12, 1985, Yarbrough joined the Shelby County Sheriff's Office, eventually retiring on August 31, 2013, with 28 years of service, earning the rank of Captain.

Captain Yarbrough was appointed the Chief of Police at Mason, Tennessee, from September 12, 2016, to February 21, 2019. He later marketed his professional services as a Law Enforcement consultant. He is the author of two books, "MISGUIDED BADGES: *A Personal Memoir*" and "BLIND DEMOCRACY: *The Shame of Hypocrisy.*"

Yarbrough, a 1961 graduate of Hamilton High School in Memphis, Tennessee, later earned a Bachelor of Arts in Criminal Justice Studies, cum laude, from LeMoyne-Owen College, a local HBCU institution. On December 16, 1996, he graduated from the FBI National Academy (FBINA), Session 187, at Quantico, Virginia, a tremendous asset to his career. The FBI National Academy, Law Enforcement Leadership Program, offered a unique 10-week educational experience for National and International police officers.

Professional memberships include the National Organization of Black Law Enforcement Executives West Tennessee Chapter (NOBLE), FBI National Academy Associates Tennessee Chapter (FBINAA), International Association of Chiefs of Police (IACP), Fraternal Order of Police (FOP) Memphis Lodge 35, Tennessee Sheriffs Association and National Sheriffs Association (NSA).

Yarbrough supports 21st-century Law Enforcement precepts and a Community Policing philosophy focused on *"the People,"* regardless of race, gender, ethnicity, economic status, political affiliation, or religious faith. He embraces mutual trust to establish relationships with proactive solutions for safer communities.

"America, STOP the Senseless Gun Violence. LIFE Matters."

"Lil Yarbrough"
1000 Miss. @ Walker
South Memphis
circa 1953

Captain
Shelby County Sheriff's Office
2004-2013

Chief
Town of Mason, Tennessee
2016-2019

ALSO FROM
D. TERRY YARBROUGH

"MISGUIDED BADGES"

MISGUIDED BADGES, reveals the boyhood experiences, career challenges, and policing philosophy of a retired Black deputy sheriff captain in Shelby County, Tennessee. It exposes systemic racism, racist attitudes, and abusive practices perpetuated within a broken American policing culture.

Available on amazon

www.ingramcontent.com/pod-product-compliance
Lightning Source LLC
Chambersburg PA
CBHW071455080526
44587CB00014B/2113